Glencoe WORLD MUSIC
A Cultural Legacy

BOB HADDAD

New York, New York   Columbus, Ohio   Woodland Hills, California   Peoria, Illinois

About the Author

This unique educational audio program was conceived, developed, and written by Bob Haddad. An ethnomusicologist and music producer, Haddad founded the Music of the World record label, which released almost 100 compact discs of traditional world music over a period of 15 years. Prior to his career in the music business, Haddad taught for 13 years on the secondary and college levels, and served as curriculum developer and teacher-trainer for various academic institutions.

He presently acts as creative consultant to educational organizations, publishers, and the music industry, and heads Owl's Head Music, a music publishing company and consultancy.

Glencoe/McGraw-Hill

A Division of The **McGraw·Hill** *Companies*

Copyright © by Owl's Head Music. All rights reserved. Published under license by The McGraw-Hill Companies, Inc. Permission is granted to reproduce the material contained herein on the condition that such material be reproduced only for classroom use and be provided to students, teachers, and families without charge. Any other reproduction, for use or sale, is prohibited without prior permission of the publisher.

Send all inquiries to:

Glencoe/McGraw-Hill
8787 Orion Place
Columbus, Ohio 43240-4027

ISBN 0-07-824189-8

Printed in the United States of America

1 2 3 4 5 6 7 8 9 10 087 08 07 06 058 04 03 02 01

Table of Contents

To the Teacher 1

To the Student 4

Music Licensors and Photo Credits 5

Complete Track Listing for the Audio Program 7

Lesson 1: Understanding the World's Music 11

Lesson 2: *Music of the United States and Canada* 13
Lesson 2: Student Worksheet 16
Lesson 2: Audio Activity 17
Exploring Regional Music Student Activity 2-A 20
Exploring Regional Music Student Activity 2-B 21

Lesson 3: *Music of Latin America* 22
Lesson 3: Student Worksheet 25
Lesson 3: Audio Activity 26
Exploring Regional Music Student Activity 3-A 29
Exploring Regional Music Student Activity 3-B 30

Lesson 4: *Music of Europe* 31
Lesson 4: Student Worksheet 34
Lesson 4: Audio Activity 35
Exploring Regional Music Student Activity 4-A 38
Exploring Regional Music Student Activity 4-B 39

Lesson 5: *Music of Russia* 40
Lesson 5: Student Worksheet 44
Lesson 5: Audio Activity 45
Exploring Regional Music Student Activity 5 47

Lesson 6: *Music of North Africa, Southwest Asia, and Central Asia* 48
Lesson 6: Student Worksheet 52
Lesson 6: Audio Activity 53
Exploring Regional Music Student Activity 6 56

Lesson 7:	*Music of Africa South of the Sahara*	57
Lesson 7:	Student Worksheet	61
Lesson 7:	Audio Activity	62

Exploring Regional Music Student Activity 7 65

Lesson 8:	*Music of South Asia*	66
Lesson 8:	Student Worksheet	70
Lesson 8:	Audio Activity	71

Exploring Regional Music Student Activity 8 74

Lesson 9:	*Music of East Asia*	75
Lesson 9:	Student Worksheet	79
Lesson 9:	Audio Activity	80

Exploring Regional Music Student Activity 9 83

Lesson 10:	*Music of Southeast Asia*	84
Lesson 10:	Student Worksheet	87
Lesson 10:	Audio Activity	88

Exploring Regional Music Student Activity 10 91

Lesson 11:	*Music of Australia and Oceania*	92
Lesson 11:	Student Worksheet	95
Lesson 11:	Audio Activity	96

Exploring Regional Music Student Activity 11 99

Glossary of Music Terms 100

Appendix of Countries 107

Answer Key 109

TO THE TEACHER

The Glencoe World Music: A Cultural Legacy *audio program has been designed to enhance your students' appreciation of geography and world cultures through music. Please read this entire section carefully before beginning to use this program in class.*

Program Components

Glencoe's *World Music: A Cultural Legacy* is a unique educational audio program, which will be fun and informative for both you and your students. The program is made up of several components, and you are encouraged to use all of them with your students to achieve maximum effect. The components are:

- Recorded examples (tracks) of regional music on CD or cassette
- An introductory student lesson
- 10 additional student lessons

    Each lesson corresponds to a different musical/cultural area or region of the world, and each of these lessons contains four parts: **1.** an essay on the music of the region; **2.** a student worksheet; **3.** audio track descriptions and questions for the students; and **4.** one or two follow-up student activity sheets. Suggested usage for each of these components is discussed in detail below (see "HOW TO USE THIS AUDIO PROGRAM").

- An answer key and additional information for teacher reference
- A selective glossary of world music terms

HOW TO USE THIS AUDIO PROGRAM

Teaching Guidelines

- Allow a minimum of one class period of approximately 45 minutes to teach the music component of each lesson.
- Pace yourself the first time you use this program and establish a system that works best for you, using a combination of class time and homework for all activities. Keep in mind that it takes 45 minutes or more to engage in all the activities for a particular lesson. Whatever your approach, it is recommended that students begin and end each lesson within a maximum period of two consecutive days.

The information below describes each program component in detail.

- **Recorded Examples**

There are 58 tracks of music, each ranging from one to three minutes in length. On the CD version, each track may be easily cued by using the controls on your CD player or remote control unit. On the cassette version, it will be best to leave the cassette at the previously played spot, rather than to rewind it each time after use. If you are using the cassette version of this program, take a few moments before class to cue-up the appropriate tracks you will use for each lesson.

- **Introductory Student Lesson**

The introductory essay "Understanding the World's Music" is meant to be read aloud in class as a warm-up to the program. There are no questions or assignments associated with this first essay. Read aloud or distribute photocopies of the page entitled "To the Student" before beginning the first lesson. This first lesson may be read and discussed by students and teachers in class, or assigned as a homework reading assignment on the day prior to discussion of this audio program. Although reading the essay is optional, it is highly recommended.

- **10 Student Lessons**

Follow these guidelines when teaching each lesson with your students.

1. **ESSAY**   (Allow 10 to 15 minutes for reading.)
   Photocopy the essay and distribute one to each of your students. Essays may be read either silently or aloud in class, or taken home as homework, along with the corresponding student worksheet for that lesson. Reading the essay and completing the student worksheet as homework may be the most practical approach when class time is limited.

2. **STUDENT WORKSHEET**   (Allow up to 10 minutes for completion.)
   Essays 2-11 each have a corresponding student worksheet. These worksheets may be completed as a class exercise, carried out silently in class as a reading/writing exercise, or assigned as homework along with the essay, to be discussed the following day or handed in for grading.

3. **AUDIO ACTIVITY**   (Allow 20-25 minutes of class time.)
   After the essays have been read and the student worksheets completed, you are ready to proceed to the core of the program, the audio material. Be sure to allow at least 25 minutes for this portion of the program, and follow these four steps:

   a. Cue up the CD or cassette to the first audio track for each lesson. On the cassette version, remember to always leave the cassette at the previously played spot.

   b. Then ask your students to read the description of the song you are about to play. A brief description of each track in the lesson is provided for both the student and the teacher.

c. Now play the audio sample. While students listen to each song, they should answer the one or two questions pertaining to that track. After the song is over, put the CD/cassette on "pause." (If a song is particularly short, or upon the students' request, you might play a track a second time for their reference.) Have students write their answers to the track questions on the photocopies or, if you are planning to use these sheets again with other students, in their notebooks or on a separate sheet of paper. Continue in this way until all tracks for each lesson are played, and all student questions are discussed.

d. Discuss the students' answers immediately after completion, either one at a time, or after the entire exercise is completed. We suggest that you review their answers aloud in class and take the opportunity to discuss the material together as a classroom activity. Keep in mind that some questions may be answered in several different ways, so encourage your students to express themselves openly.

4. FOLLOW-UP STUDENT ACTIVITIES (Allow 10-15 minutes for each activity.)
Every lesson has one or two Regional Music Student Activities, which are one-page fact sheets on topics relating to the regional music of each culture area. These activities may be used as homework assignments, for in-class discussion, or as extra credit exercises. Ask your students to write their answers on a separate sheet of paper, and collect and retain the original photocopies for future use.

• Answer Key

Answers are provided for every question on student worksheets and activity sheets. While you play each track in class, review the suggested answers to the student questions for that track. Prepare yourself with the information provided, and after the track finishes, put the CD or cassette on "pause." Then facilitate a classroom discussion for the track you just played. Base the discussion on students' responses and feelings, and on the factual information provided for each track in the answer key and essays. Continue this process until you are finished alternately playing and discussing each of the tracks in the lesson.

• Glossary

The glossary provides definitions of world music terms. Among the terms listed and described are instruments, dances, music forms, and music terms that come from many different cultures.

Glencoe designed *World Music: A Cultural Legacy*
to be informative and fun.

Enjoy the music!

TO THE STUDENT

The Glencoe *World Music: A Cultural Legacy* audio program has been designed to help you better understand and appreciate traditional and contemporary world music. As you can imagine, there is a wide variety of music on our planet, and some types of music are unlike anything else in the world. In other cases, one type of music has been influenced by another, and these influences will be heard and compared to one another.

HOW TO USE THIS PROGRAM

In this program, you will be listening to and learning about music from all over the world. There are several components of this program:

- **Essays**

You will be asked to read essays corresponding to each major culture area of the world. Your teacher may assign them for use during class or for homework. These essays contain general information about the types of music that exist in each region, and they provide you with a basic understanding of the tracks you will hear in each lesson.

- **Worksheets**

These are question-and-answer sheets that correspond to the essays, which should be completed immediately after reading each essay. Answer all questions in the spaces provided.

- **Audio Activities**

The audio activities contain descriptions of each track and questions. First you will read a description of each song. Then your teacher will play that song for you. As you listen carefully to the music, answer the questions about each song and write your answers in the spaces provided. In some cases, there are no right or wrong answers, so don't be afraid to express yourself based on what you hear and feel. Music, much like art, is interpreted by people in many different ways.

- **Activity Sheets**

These are short reading assignments that can be used in class, or as homework or extra credit. The corresponding questions can be discussed in class or handed in as homework.

This program was designed to be informative and fun.

Enjoy the music!

Music Licensors

The music in this program is reproduced under license from the following record companies.
Alula Records—Durham, NC
American Recording Productions—Farmington Hills, MI
Amiata Records—Florence, Italy
ARC Music Productions International—East Grinstead, U.K.
Blue Jackel Entertainment—Huntington, NY
Festival Distribution / Tranquila Music, Vancouver, B.C., Canada
Green Linnet Records, Inc.—Danbury, CT
Lyrichord Discs, Inc.—New York, NY
Mastertech Pty. Ltd.—Mt. Gravat, QLD, Australia
Music of the World, Ltd.—Chapel Hill, NC
New Moon Music—Somers Point, NJ
Wind Records—Taiwan, R.O.C.
World Music Institute—New York, NY

Photo Credits

Cover (tl)FPG, (tr)DigitalStock, (cl)FPG, (c)VDA/DPA/The Image Works, (cr)Corel (bl)FPG, (br)Ted Spiegel/CORBIS; **11** (l)North Carolina Museum of Art/CORBIS, (r)Harry Foster/Canadian Museum of Civilization/CORBIS; **12** Library of Congress; **13** (l)Mike Haberman/courtesy Music of the World, (r)courtesy of Chester Mahooty; **14** Artville; **15** Doug Martin; **22** Courtesy of Inkhay; **23** (l)Bob Haddad, (r)courtesy Los Pleneros de la 21; **24** Charles & Josette Lenars/CORBIS; **31** (l)C. Squared Studios/Photodisc, (r)Artville; **32** (l)John Hames/courtesy Music of the World, (r)Peter Adams/FPG; **33** (l)C. Squared Studios/Photodisc, (r)courtesy Music of the World; **40** T. O'Keefe/Photolink/Photodisc; **41** David & Peter Turnley/CORBIS; **42** R. Poderni/Sovfoto/Eastfoto/PictureQuest; **43** Jack Vartoogian; **48** AKG, Berlin/SuperStock; **49** (l)Jack Vartoogian/courtesy Music of the World, (r)courtesy The Center for Turkish Music; **50** Aaron Haupt; **51** (l)Jack Vartoogian, (r)Doug Martin; **57** Courtesy Music of the World; **58** (l)Ira Landgarten, (r)Cathy Cheney; **59** Lorraine Tipaldi; **60** Aaron Haupt; **66** C. Squared Studios/Photodisc; **67** Greg Plachta/courtesy Music of the World; **68** Sheldan Collins/CORBIS; **69** (l)courtesy Music of the World, (tr)J.F. Kenney/Ancient Art & Architecture Collection, (br)Aaron Haupt, **75** (l)CMCD/Photodisc, (r)Dean Conger/CORBIS; **76** (l)Reuters NewMedia/CORBIS, (r)Sumiyasu Miyazaki; **77** (l)Matt Meadows, (r)Lawrence Manning/CORBIS; **78** Jack Vartoogian; **84** (l)Sam-Ang Sam, (r)Bob Haddad; **85** (l)Karen Su/CORBIS, (r)Jack Vartoogian; **86** (l)Jack Vartoogian, (r)courtesy of the artist; **92** Aaron Haupt; **93** (tl)North Carolina Museum of Art/CORBIS, (r)Bettmann Archives/CORBIS, (bl)David Olsen/Stone; **94** courtesy MRA entertainment.

Additional Credits

Spoken introductions to the audio tracks read by Lue Simopoulos and Bob Haddad. Technical assistance by Michelle Carter.

The author would like to thank the following music educators for their insights:
Ray Allen, Rod Knight, Ted Levin, Elizabeth Mackinlay, William Malm, Terry E. Miller, Tim Rice, Philip Schuyler, Dan Sheehy, and Brian Silver.

COMPLETE TRACK LISTING FOR THE AUDIO PROGRAM

CD 1 — Cassette 1, Side A

THE UNITED STATES AND CANADA

Track 1   Cajun Music
Song: *"Think of Me" (Jongle A Moi)*
© ℗ 1995, Music of the World
By: Michael Doucet & BeauSoleil

Track 2   The Banjo
Song: *"Hurry!"*
© ℗ 1987, 1990, Music of the World
By: Jim Bowie

Track 3   Native American Powwow Music
Song: *"Hopi Comanche Dance"*
© ℗ 1999, Music of the World
By: Roger Mase and the 2nd Mesa

Track 4   Native American Flute
Song: *"The Land of Enchantment"*
© ℗ 1994, Music of the World
By: Cornel Pewewardy

Track 5   The Blues
Song: *"In the Darkest Hour"*
© ℗ 1994, New Moon Music
By: Nappy Brown

Track 6   Canadian Folk Music
Song: *"Gladys Ridge"*
© ℗ 1990, Tranquilla Music
By: James Keelaghan

LATIN AMERICA

Track 7   Cuba
Song: *"Pa' lo Latino"*
© ℗ 1999, Blue Jackel Entertainment
By: Tony Martínez & The Cuban Power

Track 8   Puerto Rican Folk Music
Song: *"Morena Monta en mi Guagua"*
© 1987, Music of the World; ℗ 1997, Music of the World
By: Los Pleneros de la 21

Track 9   Brazil
Song: *"Puxa Vida"*
© ℗ 1990, Music of the World
By: Tico da Costa

Track 10   Ecuador
Song: *"Corazas"*
© ℗ 1998, Music of the World
By: Inkhay

Track 11   Mexico
Song: *"El Butaquito" (Cielito Lindo)*
© ℗ 1988, 1994, Music of the World
By: Los Pregoneros del Puerto

Track 12   Peru
Song: *"Adiós Pueblo de Ayacucho"*
© ℗ 1998, Music of the World
By: Inkhay

EUROPE

Track 13   Spanish Fusion
Song: *"Fiestas en Nuevo México"*
© ℗ 1986, 1990, Music of the World
By: Carlos Lomas

World Music: A Cultural Legacy

Track 14 Sweden
Song: *"Frog Tune"*
Ⓒ ℗ 1996, Music of the World
By: Swedish Sax Septet

Track 15 Romania
Song: *"Hora: ca din caval"*
Ⓒ ℗ 1996, Music of the World
By: Musicians from the village of Marsa, Giurgiu County

Track 16 The British Isles
Song: *"The Flight"*
Ⓒ ℗ 1997, Alula Records
By: Johnny Cunningham

Track 17 Brittany
Song: *"Ar Skrilhed"*
Ⓒ 1989, Music of the World; ℗ 1996, Music of the World
By: Paul Huellou

Track 18 Bulgaria
Song: *"Ianinku"*
Ⓒ ℗ 1996, Music of the World
By: Folk Scat

Track 19 Sicily
Song: *"Danse A Trois"*
Ⓒ ℗ 1993, Music of the World
By: Enzo Rao

Cassette 1, Side B 🎧

RUSSIA

Track 20 Russia
Song: *"Kalinka"*
Ⓒ ℗ 1995, ARC Music Productions Int.
By: The Stars of St. Petersburg

Track 21 Tuva
Song: *"Taraan Taraam Dazir Sholde"*
Ⓒ ℗ 1998, Amiata Records
By: Igor Koshkendey

Track 22 Russian Choral Music
Song: *"Vysbranny Voyevodiye"*
Ⓒ ℗ 1996, ARC Music Productions Int.
By: Tolstiakov

Track 23 Russian Polka
Song: *"Polka"*
Ⓒ ℗ 1998, ARC Music Productions Int.
By: Olga Mischula and Kermash

NORTH AFRICA, SOUTHWEST ASIA, AND CENTRAL ASIA

Track 24 Morocco
Song: *"Wa yay yay Saadiya"*
Ⓒ 1989, World Music Institute; ℗ 1995, Music of the World
By: Hassan Hakmoun

Track 25 Israel
Song: *"Trance"*
Ⓒ 1998, Amiata Records; ℗ 1998 Amiata Records & Najema Music
By: Yair Dalal and the Al Ol Ensemble

Track 26 Afghanistan
Song: *"Aushari-Naghmaha-ye Logari"*
Ⓒ 1990, World Music Institute; ℗ 1996, Music of the World
By: Aziz Herawi Ensemble

Track 27 Iran
Song: *"Neyriz"*
Ⓒ ℗ 1999, Music of the World
By: Jalal and Soheil Zolfonun

Track 28 Armenia
Song: *"Tamzara"*
Ⓒ ℗ 1995, American Recording Productions
By: The Ara Topouzian Ensemble

Track 29 Turkey
Song: *"Kurdili Hicazkar Fasli"*
Ⓒ ℗ 1992, Music of the World
By: Necdet Yasar Ensemble

CD 2 — Cassette 2, Side A

AFRICA SOUTH OF THE SAHARA

Track 1 Nigeria
Song: *"Omoge Super"*
ⓒ ℗ 1991, Music of the World
By: I.K. Dairo and His Blue Spots

Track 2 Gambia
Song: *"Improvisation"*
ⓒ ℗ 1998, Music of the World
By: Yan Kuba Saho

Track 3 Zimbabwe
Song: *"Njari Makonde"*
ⓒ ℗ 1996, Music of the World
By: Ephat Mujuru and Dumisani Maraire

Track 4 Ghana
Song: *"Osoleo"*
ⓒ ℗ 1990, Music of the World
By: Obo Addy and Kukrudu

Track 5 Uganda
Song: *"Akaliba Kange"*
ⓒ 1997, James Makubuya;
℗ 1999, Music of the World
By: James Makubuya Ensemble

Track 6 Ethiopia
Song: *"Babure"*
ⓒ ℗ 2000, Music of the World
By: Seleshe Damessae

SOUTH ASIA

Track 7 Pakistan
Song: *"La Ilaha Il-Allah"*
ⓒ ℗ 1996, Green Linnet Records, Inc.
By: The Sabri Brothers

Track 8 Indian Vocal Rhythms
Song: *"Konnakkol"* (Percussion Language)
ⓒ ℗ 1997, Music of the World
By: Karnataka College of Percussion

Track 9 Bengali Folk Music
Song: *"Shola Gobe"*
ⓒ ℗ 1990, Music of the World
By: Purna Das Baul Bengali folk ensemble

Track 10 Indian Hammered Dulcimer
Song: *"Dhun in Misra Anandi"*
ⓒ ℗ 1999, Music of the World
By: Tarun Bhattacharya and Bikram Ghosh

Track 11 South Indian Flute
Song: *"Kriti: Sobhillu saptasvara"*
ⓒ ℗ 1999, Music of the World
By: N. Ramani and Trichy Sankaran

Track 12 The Sitar
Song: *"Rag Mishra Pahadi"*
ⓒ ℗ 1987, 1994, Music of the World
By: Jagdeep Singh Bedi

Track 13 North Indian Tabla
Song: *"Khandam"*
ⓒ ℗ 1999, Music of the World
By: Bikram Ghosh

EAST ASIA

Track 14 Japanese Flute
Song: *"Sagari Ha"* (Falling Leaf)
ⓒ ℗ 1991, 1994, Music of the World
By: Tadashi Tajima

Track 15 Japanese Drumming
Song: *"Hachidan Uchi Daiko"*
ⓒ ℗ 1990, Lyrichord Discs, Inc.
By: Soh Daiko

Track 16 China
Song: *"The Moon Over Wall Gate on the Frontier"*
ⓒ ℗ 1994, Wind Records
By: Chinese Instrumental Ensemble

Track 17 Korea
Song: *"Kayageum excerpt"*
ⓒ ℗ 2000, Music of the World
By: San Won Park

Track 18 Tibet
Song: *"Kul Kyon Pan"*
ⓒ ℗ 1998, Amiata Media Srl.
By: Monks of the Sera Jé Monastery

SOUTHEAST ASIA

Track 19 The *Khene* From Laos
Song: *"Lam Ploen"*
ⓒ 1989, World Music Institute; ℗ 1996, Music of the World
By: Khamvong Insixiengmai Ensemble

Track 20 Vietnamese Folk Music
Song: *"Do Doc Do Ngang"* (Boat Song)
ⓒ 1989, World Music Institute; ℗ 1997, Music of the World
By: Phong Nguyen

Track 21 Javanese Gamelan
Song: *"Ladrang Galagothang"*
ⓒ ℗ 1989, 1994, Music of the World
By: Palace musicians and singers

Track 22 Drumming From Vietnam
Song: *"Drum Improvisation"*
ⓒ 1989, World Music Institute; ℗ 1997, Music of the World
By: Phong Nguyen

Track 23 Cambodia
Song: *"Toch Yum"*
ⓒ ℗ 1997, Music of the World
By: Sam Ang Sam

Track 24 Laotian Folk Music
Song: *"Lam Ban Xok"*
ⓒ 1989, World Music Institute;
℗ 1996, Music of the World
By: Khamvong Insixiengmai Ensemble

AUSTRALIA AND OCEANIA

Track 25 Australian Fusion
Song: *"Spirits of the Sky"*
ⓒ ℗ 1997, Mastertech Pty Ltd
By: Uluru: Rhythms of the Rock

Track 26 Samoa
Song: *"E keli"*
ⓒ ℗ 1997, ARC Music Productions Int.
By: Te Vaka

Track 27 Folk Music From Vanuatu
Song: *"Vanuatu"*
ⓒ ℗ 1995, ARC Music Productions Int.
By: Fenes String Band

Track 28 The Didgeridoo
Song: *"Didgeridoo Introduction"*
ⓒ ℗ 2000, Mastertech Pty Ltd
By: Harry Wilson

Track 29 Australian Folk Music
Song: *"Bound for South Australia"*
ⓒ ℗ 1996, 1999, Mastertech Pty Ltd
By: The Aussie Bush Band

Name _____ Date _____ Class _____

Lesson 1
Understanding the World's Music

DIRECTIONS: Read the information below, and be prepared to discuss it in class.

Music is an important element of cultural identity. It directly reflects the society from which it comes. Much like language, music is continuously evolving, changing, and absorbing new influences. In this way, it is a living art, a true expression of cultural identity.

Geographic Factors

To understand and appreciate the various types of music in the world today, it can be helpful to view them within the contexts of geography and history. Natural barriers such as mountain ranges and bodies of water have helped some cultures to resist outside influences, so music in remote areas is often more pure or traditional. In the past, an open area with easy access to transportation may have been more exposed to outside influences, and the music in this type of region may have changed or evolved at a quicker rate than in more isolated areas.

Historical Transformations

Just as geography has influenced music development, history has also played an important role. For the most part, colonial European powers brought their own music to the lands they conquered, and often banned traditional forms of native music. At the same time, many Native American and African people did their best to keep their traditional music alive. Over time, these non-European styles of music influenced and gave birth to new forms of music, most of which are still heard today.

Early Central African dance rattle

Influences Across Cultures

To understand this type of musical "transculturalism," let's consider the interesting case of Africa. When European settlers colonized Africa, a region rich in music and cultural expression, certain styles of African music slowly became "westernized." Today's folk music from the Cape Verde islands off the northwest coast of Africa, for

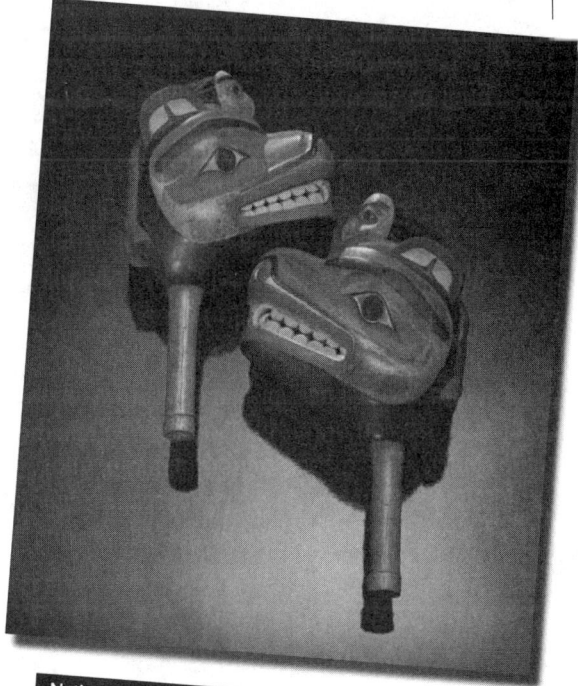
Native American rattles

World Music: A Cultural Legacy   **11**

Lesson 1

example, sounds very similar to the traditional music of Portugal, and is sung in Creole, a language derived from Portuguese. Just as European musical influences were taking root on African soil, though; enslaved Africans were bringing traditional African instruments and music into the Americas.

In coastal areas of Latin America, new Africanized music forms were born. In the Caribbean, African drums and rhythms mixed with Spanish strings and harmonies, eventually leading to music such as merengue and salsa. In Louisiana, African rhythms mixed with Native American and French music and gave way to Cajun music. Brazilian samba and bossa nova have their roots in African rhythms. In the American South, African singing and improvisation gave way to gospel music, blues, jazz, and even rock and roll. As proof that music is a living art, today's African musicians have been influenced by modern music such as jazz, salsa, and rock. In other words, modern African musicians are now being influenced by music from other cultures that their own ancestors helped to bring about!

This Music Program

When you listen to the music selections in this program, try to keep an open mind. Remember that what may sound strange to you can sound perfectly normal to another person in another land. Try to listen for the similarities and differences in the music you're hearing as compared to the music that you are familiar with in your own life. Listen for recurring patterns, and try to identify them in your written responses and classroom discussions. As you listen to each selection, allow the music to sink in for a few moments, and try to imagine what it would be like to be among the musicians in their own country. If you allow yourself to be transported by the music in this way, you'll be one step closer to appreciating the great variety of human cultures that inhabit our planet.

Enslaved Africans working in cotton fields

12 World Music: A Cultural Legacy

Name _____ Date _____ Class _____

Lesson 2
Music of the United States and Canada

DIRECTIONS: Read the information below, and use it to complete the Lesson 2 Student Worksheet.

Music in North America directly reflects the diverse population of the region. North American music ranges from early colonial songs to the modern tunes of today. European, African, and Native American traditions are the major influences that have made strong contributions to the music of this region.

Native American Music

Thousands of years before the arrival of the Europeans to the Americas, Native Americans had developed a very strong musical tradition. Among Native Americans, music was a part of everyday life, and had strong ties to spirituality and reverence. Across the continent, different Native American groups used songs and dances for hunting, waging war, planting and harvesting, calling for rain, celebrating births and funerals, and for many other social activities.

Throughout the region, there are several common characteristics of Native American music. Singers usually perform in groups, rather than sing in solo fashion. The music usually consists of one or more drums and sometimes shakers, rattles, and bells. Songs often tell stories about animals, gods, and sacred places. The singing is often performed in "vocables," or vowel sounds with no real meaning.

Sadly, much traditional music was lost when the Europeans arrived, conquered Native American nations, and destroyed native cultures on the North American continent. In recent years, however, intertribal powwows have become very popular throughout the United States and Canada, and have helped to keep the ancient traditions alive. Powwows feature traditional singing and dancing, competitions, and native arts. Many are open to the general public.

Cornel Pewewardy (left) is of Kiowa and Comanche lineage. He plays the Indian Plains flute. Chester Mahooty's music (right) reflects the culture of the Zuni nation of Arizona and New Mexico.

World Music: A Cultural Legacy

Name _____ Date _____ Class _____

Lesson 2

European Influences

When Europeans arrived in the Americas, they brought music and instruments from their homelands with them. The earliest settlers spread out to eastern Canada and to central and southern areas of the United States. Many arrived from England and Scotland, and brought with them folk songs that recounted tales of kingdoms and village life. Early American folk songs sprang up from this tradition and were based on stories of local events, adventures, conflicts, love, and other daily concerns. French people who settled in Quebec also had rich folk singing and fiddling traditions.

Frontier songs and fiddle tunes became very popular in rural communities, especially in the Cape Breton region of Nova Scotia. The French-speaking Acadian people found their way down to Louisiana, and took with them a distinct song tradition of waltzes and two-steps played on the fiddle and accordion. This gave way to the Cajun music of today, popular in Louisiana and at folk festivals and concert halls across America.

Farther west, along the Texas/Mexican border, another accordion-based style exists today, known as "Norteño" or Tex-Mex music. This lively music combines Spanish lyrics and song forms with bouncy German polka rhythms.

American country music also had its beginnings during this period. Country music has clear links to British ballads, Native American songs, and Scots-Irish fiddle tunes. Settlers in Appalachia originally sang in a tense, high-pitched style that can still be heard in some contemporary country music. All along, the fiddle continued to be very popular, and thanks to its portability and strong sound, it was the perfect instrument to accompany country dancing. A strong repertoire of country music developed over the years, using guitars, mandolins, and bass. These days, with electric instruments and modern innovations, country music continues to expand and is popular in many areas of the United States and Canada.

African Roots

The first enslaved Africans brought to the United States a culture rich in music, song, and dance. Although plantation slaveholders attempted to ban and suppress this ritual music, enslaved Africans managed to keep their traditions alive. They also began to adapt their music to certain European instruments and music forms. This mixing of African and European/American styles is still evident in much of the folk music of the southern United States.

Gospel music is a type of religious singing that emerged in northern and midwestern urban areas of the United States around the turn of the twentieth century. Its roots can be traced back to the rural folk music of the American South. The moaning sound of old spirituals, the tight vocal harmonies of minstrel groups and quartets, and the rhythmic influence of early jazz and blues all contributed to the evolution of African American gospel music. Gospel music continues to flourish today, and it has become recognized as a major expression of African American culture.

A modern fiddle

Lesson 2

Blues music, as we know it today, was also developed in African American communities around the turn of the century. Work songs, field hollers, country dances, and spirituals all influenced the earliest forms of the blues. The structure of European music's sung verses and the use of guitar as accompaniment also played an important role. Blues varies in form around the United States, and there are several important regions with different styles. "Delta blues" is performed in the south-central United States, with the Mississippi delta as a focal point. The music here can often be percussive in nature, with dense rhythms and raspy vocals. "Piedmont" blues developed in the southeastern states, and is characterized by a finger-picking style strongly influenced by old-time or "hillbilly" music. "Chicago blues" has a pulsating, modern electric sound, and is often heard in midwestern urban areas. Memphis, Tennessee was also an important early center for the development of blues. The world's most famous blues artist, B.B. King, developed his style in the Memphis area by incorporating bits of jazz and using a singing style inspired by spirituals and gospel music.

Deborah Coleman's unique blend of blues and rock was influenced by Jimi Hendrix, Led Zeppelin, Muddy Waters, and Bessie Smith.

In a similar way, jazz evolved from a mixture of early African American music and European styles and instruments. "Ragtime" was a popular music of the early 1900s with strong syncopated rhythms. Other types of jazz followed, with names like Swing, Bebop, Big Band, Dixieland, and more recently "Smooth" Jazz. No matter what type of jazz it is, improvisation (creating music spontaneously) is always central to the main theme.

In the early 1950s, the mixing of white country music with African American "rhythm and blues" produced the beginnings of a music that came to be known as "rock and roll." Rock and roll evolved into modern-day rock, taking on more modern arrangements and utilizing louder, electric instruments. Other modern forms of music such as rap and hip-hop all have their roots in earlier forms of American music.

What is most significant about the music of North America is the mixing of different cultural styles and borrowing of elements from one type of music to another. This region has produced a dazzling array of music, drawn from diverse cultural influences and spanning many years.

Name _____ Date _____ Class _____

Lesson 2

The United States and Canada
Student Worksheet

DIRECTIONS: Read about the music of the United States and Canada on pages 13–15. Then using the essay and, if necessary, your geography text as references, answer the following questions in the spaces provided.

1. What language do Cajuns sing in? _____

2. Name another type of music in the United States that is not sung in English.

   _____

3. Many blues songs express feelings of sadness and hard times. Which turn of the century social conditions in the southern United States might have inspired African Americans to create blues music?

   _____

   _____

4. Blues was originally an African American music, but people of other races have also come to enjoy it. Why do you think the blues appeals to people of different ethnic backgrounds?

   _____

   _____

5. Much Native American music was lost as Europeans settled North America. Why do you think this happened?

   _____

   _____

6. How have Native Americans revived their traditional styles of song and dance in recent years?

   _____

   _____

7. Name several types of early jazz and one modern type.

   _____

   _____

16   World Music: A Cultural Legacy

Name _____ Date _____ Class _____

Lesson 2

Music of the United States and Canada

DIRECTIONS: As you listen to the music of the United States and Canada on Disc One, Tracks 1-6 (Cassette 1, Side A), answer the questions that follow in the spaces provided.

TRACK 1 CAJUN MUSIC

 Song "Think of Me" (Jongle A Moi)
Ⓒ Ⓟ 1995, Music of the World
By: Michael Doucet & BeauSoleil

This song is based on an original composition by J.B. Fusilier, an early Cajun fiddler who recorded Louisiana Cajun music in the 1930s.

1. Of all the instruments in this song, which is the most prominent?

   _____

   _____

2. Two-steps have two beats and waltzes have three. Try to count the beats in this song by lightly tapping your foot or hand on the desk. Do you think it is a two-step or a waltz?

   _____

   _____

TRACK 2 THE BANJO

 Song "Hurry"
Ⓒ Ⓟ 1987, 1990, Music of the World
By: Jim Bowie

This is a modern composition performed on banjo, based on traditional American banjo music. The fast, upbeat tempo has a traditional bluegrass flavor.

1. The notes in this song are played lightning fast. Do you think the musician is strumming the strings in one direction, or with up and down motions? Why?

   _____

   _____

   _____

World Music: A Cultural Legacy   17

Name _____ Date _____ Class _____

Lesson 2

TRACK 3 — NATIVE AMERICAN POWWOW MUSIC

Song: "Hopi Comanche Dance"
© ℗ 1999, Music of the World
By: Roger Mase and the 2nd Mesa

This early winter dance gives thanks for the moisture of winter, which prepares the soil for spring. The text is sung in vocables (vowel-sounds without meaning) and the phrase endings are similar to those of Plains war dance songs.

1. In addition to the drum, what other instruments do you hear?

   _____

   _____

   _____

   _____

TRACK 4 — NATIVE AMERICAN FLUTE

Song: "The Land of Enchantment"
© ℗ 1994, Music of the World
By: Cornel Pewewardy

This song is about the Comanche and their adventures in what is now the state of New Mexico. During the early 1900s, Native American warriors would venture into New Mexico in search of wild horses.

1. List some words to describe the mood of this song.

   _____

   _____

   _____

   _____

   _____

   _____

   _____

18   World Music: A Cultural Legacy

Name _____ Date _____ Class _____

Lesson 2

TRACK 5 | THE BLUES

Song "In the Darkest Hour"
© ℗ 1994, New Moon Music
By: Nappy Brown

This is a modern blues composition describing just how bad things can be when you are without the one you love. "The darkest hour is just before the break of day."

1. After each line that is sung by the singer, which instrument plays a response? What kind of effect does this have on the song?

   _____
   _____
   _____
   _____
   _____

TRACK 6 | CANADIAN FOLK MUSIC

Song "Gladys Ridge"
© ℗ 1990, Tranquilla Music
By: James Keelaghan

This is a modern folk song about life, inspired by a beautiful, ambling hill just south of Calgary, Alberta.

1. There are two musical elements that repeat several times in this song. One is the plucked melody that begins the song. What is the other element?

   _____
   _____

2. What effect do repetitive elements in a song have on the listener?

   _____
   _____
   _____

World Music: A Cultural Legacy

Name _____ Date _____ Class _____

Lesson 2

Exploring Regional Music
Student Activity 2-A

DIRECTIONS: Read the information below, then answer the questions that follow on a separate sheet of paper and be prepared to discuss your answers in class.

CAJUN MUSIC

West of New Orleans, Louisiana, lies a large chunk of the state that is commonly referred to as "Cajun country." The Cajuns are descendants of French settlers who arrived on the shores of Nova Scotia (then called Acadia), Canada in the eighteenth century. As a result of disputes and cultural pressures, the British colonizers forced the Acadians to leave the area. Some were sent back to France and others, after years of wandering, found their way to Louisiana, which was at that time a French colony. Here, they established themselves as the dominant culture of the region and have made themselves known for keeping alive their French language and heritage, their spicy cooking, and their typical Cajun music.

Cajun music originated with fiddles, and then later incorporated the accordion, which the Acadians borrowed from Germany; the guitar from Spain; percussion and syncopated rhythms from enslaved Africans; and the steady beat and hollers from Native American peoples. The most popular Cajun songs are romantic slow waltzes and lively, bouncy two-steps. Just as a spicy gumbo has many different herbs and seasonings, musical styles from several cultures combined to bring about what is known today as Cajun music.

Cajun music's more modern cousin is called zydeco, and it sometimes borrows a bit from blues, rock and roll, and anything else that will keep the people on the dance floor. Many basic Cajun tunes, waltzes, and two-steps are played in zydeco, and songs are sung in French and English.

An important instrument for both Cajun and zydeco music is the washboard. This instrument is modeled after the old metal washboards people washed their clothes with before the development of modern appliances. When used as a percussion instrument, the washboard is strapped to the musician's chest, and scraped up and down, producing a sharp rasping noise.

In recent years modern Cajun and zydeco music have been popularized in movies, on pop albums, and in television commercials. The traditional songs of the French Acadians are also very much alive and can still be heard in parts of Louisiana and East Texas.

An example of Cajun music can be heard on Glencoe's "World Music: A Cultural Legacy" audio program—Disc One, Track 1 (Cassette 1, Side A).

QUESTIONS TO CONSIDER

1. How did the Cajun people find their way to Louisiana?

2. Why do you think Cajun music and culture has stayed so strong over the years?

3. Name two things that are shared between Cajun and zydeco music.

Name _____ Date _____ Class _____

Exploring Regional Music
Student Activity 2-B

DIRECTIONS: Read the information below, then answer the questions that follow on a separate sheet of paper and be prepared to discuss your answers in class.

NATIVE AMERICAN MUSIC

The term *Native Americans* is used to describe the many nations of native peoples in the Americas whose ancestors were the first to arrive in this region around 30,000 years ago. These first Americans developed customs, religions, languages, and music that are unique.

A main characteristic of Native American music is that it is performed almost entirely through singing. This singing is mostly done in groups although some traditions also allow for solo singing. Generally speaking, harmony is not used, and groups of singers sing the same notes together in unison. Singing styles are generally strong—songs tend to be loud and may feature animal calls, whoops, and other cries. The rhythm of most Native American music usually stays constant throughout the piece. Traditionally singing is carried out by men, but there are also storytelling songs that are sung by both men and women. There are also a few genres of songs specifically for women.

An important characteristic of Native American singing is that very often, real words are not used. Untranslatable syllables called "vocables" often shape the entire structure of the song. Of course, there are also translatable words in some Native American songs, but these words often refer to animals, gods, and sacred places.

As a whole, Native American people share similar types of dances, ceremonies, and spiritual beliefs, but there are also sharp distinctions among groups. The Plains nations share a ceremony that pays homage to the earth, sun, and wind for good health and a plentiful supply of buffalo. The singing is done in a very high, almost screeching voice. The Iroquois of the Northeast have a ceremony that focuses on giving thanks. The singing at these events is characterized by high calls, and the songs sometimes change speeds before ending. Among the coastal nations of the Pacific Northwest and southwest Canada, individual compositions may praise a deceased member of the community or boast about a family's wealth and status. In general, however, songs that relay personal feelings are rare.

Modern Native Americans often perform country and western music. There are Native American rock groups, New Age music groups, and groups that perform hymn singing among the various Christian denominations. These new music forms coexist with the older forms, and together they shape the musical backbone of modern Native American life.

An example of Native American powwow music can be heard on Glencoe's "World Music: A Cultural Legacy" audio program—Disc One, Track 3 (Cassette 1, Side A). The Native American flute is featured on Track 4.

QUESTIONS TO CONSIDER

1. Name two ways in which Native American music is unlike other types of music.
2. Although today's young Native Americans enjoy modern music, the music of their ancestors still lives on. Why do you think this is so?

World Music: A Cultural Legacy

Name _____ Date _____ Class _____

Lesson 3
Music of Latin America

DIRECTIONS: Read the information below, and use it to complete the Lesson 3 Student Worksheet.

Latin America has a wide variety of musical traditions, and each style of music reflects the cultural makeup of each country in the region. The three major groups of people that came together to form the population of Latin America are the native (indigenous) peoples; the Europeans (from Spain, Portugal, and other countries); and the Africans who were forced to immigrate because of the slave trade. If you consider the wide geographical differences that exist in this region, and imagine the different combinations of cultural backgrounds that came into being here, it is not surprising that there is such a wide variety of music in Latin America today.

Native American Sources

Several hundred distinct languages and cultures existed in the Americas many years before European explorers arrived, beginning in 1492. Chroniclers wrote about the rich cultures, religions, languages, and music traditions they encountered on their journeys. Although hundreds of years have passed since the days of the Spanish conquest, many European cultural traditions are still alive in Latin America.

The Aztec civilization of central Mexico was practically destroyed within 20 years after the invasion of Hernán Cortés. From the remains of temple paintings and ancient manuscripts with detailed drawings, though, we know that these proud people used wooden drums, flutes, and all sorts of percussion instruments, many made from human bones. The Maya of Central America played long trumpets made of wood or metal, whistle flutes, and ocarinas (enclosed wind instruments with several holes). The Inca of the South American highlands commonly used bamboo flutes and panpipes. These instruments are still in use today.

Inkhay is a Quechua word that that means "to feed a fire." Inkhay is also a group of Andean musicians whose music reflects the proud heritage of the Andean region.

Traditional music from Peru, Bolivia, and Ecuador share many characteristics common among the native inhabitants of this region who date back thousands of years before the European conquest.

Lesson 3

Peruvian musician playing a mandolin made from an armadillo shell.

The gauchos of the vast Argentine plains (pampas) favor the common six-string Spanish guitar, but the rhythms and melodies they play are very typically Argentinean. The most well-known traditional music style from Argentina is the tango, a romantic music form that evolved exclusively in Argentina. The tango became very popular in the early twentieth century, when it spread to neighboring countries, Europe, and the United States.

In Mexico one of the most characteristic types of music is called *mariachi*. Mariachi musicians use string and brass instruments, accompanied by tight vocal harmonies. Although early Spanish music strongly influenced its creation, mariachi music went on to develop a distinctive Mexican flair. Today mariachi music is identified all over the world as a unique Mexican music tradition.

Innovations From Europe

Europeans from Spain, Portugal, Great Britain, the Netherlands, and other countries arrived to colonize the Americas in the 1700s and 1800s. They brought with them the instruments and music they had played back home. Before their arrival, making music with strings was probably not practiced in the Americas, and the idea of harmony (playing or singing several notes at one time) was not common. These innovations, along with the numerous new instruments Europeans introduced to the Americas, had an enormous impact on the way regional music styles evolved in Latin America.

The instrument that probably had the strongest influence on the Americas was the guitar. Native populations quickly began to play guitar, and adapted the concept of strings suspended over a fretboard in order to create new hybrid instruments. One such instrument, the *charango,* is a small mandolin born in the Andes with a body made of an armadillo shell. Music from the Andes is played in both Spanish and Native American-derived rhythms; it combines native and European instruments; and is sung in the native languages of Quechua and Aymara as well as in Spanish.

Los Pleneros de la 21, based in "El Barrio" in East Harlem, New York City, proudly performs the Afro-Puerto Rican traditions of the *bomba* and *plena*. The roots of their music come from the days when Spanish colonists brought enslaved West Africans to work in Puerto Rico's sugarcane fields.

World Music: A Cultural Legacy

Lesson 3

African Influences

Descendants of Africans from many ethnic backgrounds were brought to Latin America as slaves (especially to the Caribbean islands and Brazil). These people played a major role in shaping the music that would evolve in these regions. Consider, for example, the marimba, a xylophone made of wooden keys and suspended tubes or gourds that amplify the sound. This instrument is found throughout Central America and in southern Mexico. Its direct ancestor, the *balafon*, is still in use today in many countries of West Africa.

Music from the eastern Mexican state of Veracruz is very lively and features many string instruments, which were originally introduced by the Spaniards. The syncopated rhythms they play, though, can be traced back to the African inhabitants of this coastal area, and to a well-known West African harp known as the *kora*.

In Portuguese-speaking Brazil, popular types of music such as samba and bossa nova owe much of their special character to African cultural strains present in that country for hundreds of years. Music associated with *candomblé*, religious rituals that combine healing and magic, are still sung in Yoruba, the language of Nigeria.

A Central American musician plays the marimba.

In Puerto Rico, the *plena* is typically performed in African style by several people playing tambourines, called *panderetas*, along with other African-inspired drums and percussion. The song form is set in the African "call-and-response" style, whereby a leader sings a phrase and the entire group sings a response.

Cuban rumba and Santería music, Dominican merengue, and other local music forms are also African in origin but are now enjoyed far beyond their national boundaries. Salsa, the hypnotic dance music of Cuban and Puerto Rican origin, has at its source basic African rhythmic principles. Salsa utilizes drums and percussion such as congas and bongos, which were born of African traditions, and are now popular all over the world.

In the English-speaking Caribbean, steel drums or "pans" as they are called locally, are the most characteristic instruments. Entire orchestras of pans were developed in Trinidad and are played largely by Afro-Caribbean people throughout the region. The type of music played on steel drums is called *calypso,* which became very popular from the 1950s onward. A more recent popular music from this region is called *soca* (from "soul-calypso").

As you listen to the audio tracks for Lesson 3, notice the musical contrasts and diversity in the music of Latin America. The region's many cultural origins and the creativity of its people have led to the creation of diverse and exciting music forms, now known all over the world.

Name _____ Date _____ Class _____

Lesson 3

Latin America
Student Worksheet

DIRECTIONS: Read about the music of Latin America on pages 22–24. Then using the essay and, if necessary, your geography text as references, answer the following questions in the spaces provided.

1. What are the three major ethnic groups that have contributed to Latin American culture?

2. Describe a musical contribution from each group.

3. Name and describe a hybrid musical instrument found in Latin America.

4. In which region of Latin America are panpipes most common? Name two important countries from this region.

5. What are gauchos and where are they found?

6. Which musical instrument do gauchos have in common with their counterparts in the United States?

World Music: A Cultural Legacy   25

Name _____ Date _____ Class _____

Lesson 3

Music of Latin America

DIRECTIONS: As you listen to the music of Latin America on Disc One, Tracks 7-12 (Cassette 1, Side A), answer the questions that follow in the spaces provided.

TRACK 7 CUBA

Song "Pa' lo Latino"
ⓒ ⓟ 1999, Blue Jackel Entertainment
By: Tony Martínez & The Cuban Power

This composition is based on Cuban *son* (a traditional music form). Played with lots of brass instruments and percussion, it has a strong Latin jazz flavor.

1. Name all the instruments you hear in this piece.

   _____

   _____

2. If you tap your feet or move your head to the rhythm, do you notice anything unusual when the horns come in?

   _____

   _____

TRACK 8 PUERTO RICAN FOLK MUSIC

Song "Morena Monta en mi Guagua"
ⓒ 1987, Music of the World;
ⓟ 1997, Music of the World
By: Los Pleneros de la 21

This is a folk song about a boy who asks a dark-haired girl to go for a ride with him in his car. This song has strong African and Spanish influences.

1. In the introduction to this song, which instruments do you think are African in origin and which one is Spanish?

   _____

2. The vocal style is called "call-and-response." Describe it in your own words.

   _____

   _____

26   World Music: A Cultural Legacy

Lesson 3

TRACK 9 BRAZIL

Song "Puxa Vida"
 © ℗ 1990, Music of the World
 By: Tico da Costa

This song is about all the things a husband does for his wife. Even though he doesn't like to, he goes shopping, washes the dishes, cleans the house, and so on, just because he loves her.

1. What are some words that describe the mood of this music?

___

TRACK 10 ECUADOR

Song "Corazas"
 © ℗ 1998, Music of the World
 By: Inkhay

This is an ancient Ecuadorian rhythm called *yumbo*, which is played on several *payas*, a type of pentatonic panpipe.

1. Does this song sound native or influenced by music from Europe? Explain your answer.

___

2. What does the drumbeat remind you of?

___

World Music: A Cultural Legacy

Name _____ Date _____ Class _____

Lesson 3

TRACK 11 — MEXICO

Song: "El Butaquito" (Cielito Lindo)
© ℗ 1988, 1994, Music of the World
By: Los Pregoneros del Puerto

This song is the original version of the popular tune "Cielito Lindo," which originated in the Mexican state of Veracruz, near the Gulf of Mexico.

1. Does this song contain a call-and-response vocal form? Explain your answer.

   _____

   _____

   _____

2. When the harper plays a solo, do you think it is a planned-out melody, or do you think the musician is improvising on the spot? Explain.

   _____

   _____

TRACK 12 — PERU

Song: "Adiós Pueblo de Ayacucho"
© ℗ 1998, Music of the World
By: Inkhay

This is a well-known song from Peru that includes harp, *quena* flutes, *charango* (armadillo-shell mandolin), and guitar.

1. Do you think the harp was developed in Peru or brought to South America from Spain?

   _____

   _____

2. Are there one or two flutes playing in this song? What makes you think so?

   _____

   _____

   _____

World Music: A Cultural Legacy

Name _____ Date _____ Class _____

Lesson 3

Exploring Regional Music
Student Activity 3-A

DIRECTIONS: Read the information below, then answer the questions that follow on a separate sheet of paper. Be prepared to discuss your answers in class.

TRADITIONAL FLUTES OF THE ANDES

Many centuries before the first conquistadors sailed toward the Americas, traditional music played an important role in society throughout Latin America, especially in the mountainous region of South America known as the altiplano, or high plain. The rugged Andes mountain range pushes its way through five countries and spans thousands of miles, but it is in Peru and Bolivia where some of the oldest music of the Western Hemisphere originated. In early times, people used music for religious and ceremonial purposes. They probably did not use music for recreation and social enjoyment as we do now. In addition to voice, only percussion and wind instruments were utilized. To this day, the single most identifying sound of music from the Andes region is that of flutes and panpipes.

The most common wind instruments were bamboo flutes called *quenas*, although ceremonial *quenas* made of animal and human bone have been unearthed in temple excavations. The peoples of this region crafted panpipes called *zampoñas*, or *sikus*, of bamboo in different sizes and pitches. The *quena* and *zampoña* traditions are still very much alive today in the Andes, and these instruments are played by Andean folk groups in most major cities around the world.

To make these wind instruments, individual bamboo stalks are precisely cut and lashed together in straight lines with woolen string and strips of bamboo. In some cases, the notes of a given scale alternate from one set of pipes to another so that in order for a complete melody to be played, two people must play two separate sets of pipes. These bamboo wind instruments can be as small as a few inches long, or as large as up to three or four feet tall. Keeping in mind that the air is quite thin at very high altitudes, it is not surprising to learn that these mountain dwelling people have a larger thoracic capacity than that of lowland inhabitants. Andean musicians need all the help they can get in order to play the giant, mysterious-sounding panpipes that are still in use today.

An example of Andean panpipe music can be heard on Glencoe's "World Music: A Cultural Legacy" audio program—Disc One, Track 10 (Cassette 1, Side A).

QUESTIONS TO CONSIDER

1. Name all the countries that share the Andes mountain range.

2. What are some ways in which ancient music from this region differs from the modern music of our times?

World Music: A Cultural Legacy

Lesson 3

Exploring Regional Music
Student Activity 3-B

DIRECTIONS: Read the information below, then answer the questions that follow on a separate sheet of paper. Be prepared to discuss your answers in class.

AFRO-CARIBBEAN SANTERÍA MUSIC

The Spanish colonization of the Americas, which began in the early 1500s, effectively destroyed the lives of the native peoples of the Caribbean region. By the middle of the eighteenth century, European colonists enslaved and imported massive numbers of West Africans to work in bondage on sugar plantations. By 1840 Africans accounted for more than half of the population of many Caribbean islands. They preserved their identity in associations called *cabildos,* and they secretly worshiped the African gods of their ancestors.

Today the Afro-Cuban religion known as Santería honors a variety of deities known as *orishas,* which are also associated with Roman Catholic saints. Santería music was traditionally used only in private ceremonies, but in recent years it has become much more available to the general public through recordings and concerts.

Santería music is performed using only drums, percussion, and voices. The double-headed drums are called *batá,* and the shakers (*shékeres*) are made of dried gourds and beads. The drumming rhythms are very complex, and they interact with each other in a certain sequence within the religious ceremony. There are three different sizes of sacred *batá* drums. Some people believe that when the *batá* are played together, they create rhythms that evoke spirits who descend and take possession of devotees. Followers believe that the largest drum, *iyá,* communicates directly with the *orishas,* each of whom has his or her own color and identifying rhythms. This drum also enters into direct conversation with the middle-sized drum. The smallest drum plays a rhythmic pattern that changes when it hears a signal from the *iyá*. The singing is almost entirely in Yoruba, the language of Nigeria, and is carried out in a call-and-response style, whereby the lead singer is regularly answered by a chorus.

In Cuba today, a strong percentage of the population maintains a faith based on Santería, and dances and musical ceremonies are performed in honor of the major deities. To a lesser extent, Santería is also still practiced in Puerto Rico and in French-speaking Haiti, where these same Nigerian and West African traditions were transformed into vodoun (voodoo), which is widely in use today.

An example of Puerto Rican folk music can be heard on Glencoe's "World Music: A Cultural Legacy" audio program—Disc One, Track 8 (Cassette 1, Side A).

QUESTIONS TO CONSIDER

1. Describe how Afro-Cuban drums play separately, yet together.

2. What is Yoruba, and when and where is it used in Latin America today?

Name _____ Date _____ Class _____

Lesson 4

Music of Europe

DIRECTIONS: Read the information below, and use it to complete the Lesson 4 Student Worksheet.

The organization, composition, and public performance of music in Europe dates back several millennia. Europe today is considered one of the strongest cultural areas to have fostered music and the arts. What is now known as classical music was developed and nurtured here many hundreds of years ago. What many people don't realize, though, is that earlier music from other cultures influenced much of the traditional music of Europe.

Outside Influences

Many thousands of years ago, Arab and Turkish influences shaped the social, economic, and cultural fabric of Europe. Many of these influences reached the European continent from North Africa by way of the Mediterranean Sea. If we try to understand Europe not as an isolated continent, but rather as the western part of the huge Eurasian landmass, it can help us to understand many aspects of its musical and cultural traditions.

The ancient Greeks are credited with establishing the basis of modern European culture and the foundations of music in the region. They first learned about mathematics, philosophy, and music, however, through their contacts with the great Egyptian empire. Early Christian music called Gregorian chant flourished throughout Europe in the Middle Ages, yet this music had its origins in the Middle East. Bowed instruments such as cellos and violins reached a point of great refinement in the classical music of Europe, but they were based on instruments already in widespread use in Asia. Europeans borrowed most percussion and reed instruments from the Turks, and developed the guitar based on the concept of the Middle Eastern lute. Before cultural contact with Asia, Europeans probably had only a limited range of wind instruments such as flutes, natural horns, and bagpipes with which to play music.

Geographic Identities

The spreading of Christianity gave Europeans a common set of religious and ethical values. Despite the fact that Europeans share a tradition of classical music, similar instruments, tunings, and harmonies, there are also widely divergent customs, cuisines, languages, and political systems in Europe. Consequently, a great variety of music styles and dances may be found literally within a few miles of one another. Part of the reason for such a wide variety of cultural expression is the geography of the region. If you look at a map of Europe, you will see that it is an area of many islands and peninsulas divided by bodies of water. There are also large mountain ranges, which physically

The guitar (right) is an adaptation of the lute (left).

World Music: A Cultural Legacy 31

Name _____ Date _____ Class _____

Lesson 4

Flamenco combines acoustic guitar playing, singing, chanting, dancing, and staccato hand clapping. Flamenco guitarists, like Carlos Lomas of Spain, dancers, and singers often perform to shouts of *olé* or *baile* from the audience.

traditional music in Europe. In Greece, Bulgaria, Scandinavia, and other regions, however, unusual rhythms using 7, 9, 11, and 15 beats may be found. Concepts of harmony may also vary widely from one region to another. Bosnia, for example, has preserved an ancient type of singing based on singing notes that are very close to each other. The effect is jarring and dissonant, and might not be considered pleasing by other European cultures, yet the Bosnians strive for this musical sound and enjoy the clashing effect it creates for listeners.

separate and isolate regions from each other, even within national borders. Before the development of modern transportation and open travel from one political region to another, natural barriers such as mountain ranges and oceans kept many areas separated from outside influences, and minimized cultural blending. In this way, individual customs, languages, and music remained unique from one region to another. Over the past hundred years or so, modernization has helped to blend different cultures in Europe, but Europeans still hold fast to local customs and national and regional traditions. In a rapidly changing Europe, one that introduced the euro as a single currency for many nations, it is still important for Europeans to embrace and foster local customs, languages, and music as a statement of their unique identities.

A Variety of Musical Expressions

The great majority of European folk music uses either a two-beat or a three-beat rhythm, and the use of harmony (playing or singing more than one note at the same time) is common to most

Despite modern times and the previously mentioned unifying features, there is an incredible variety of music in Europe today. In Portugal, a whole repertoire of sad songs evolved from the widows of fishers and sailors who were lost at sea. The widows, in mourning and dressed in black, would wail plaintive melodies while staring out into the ocean. In Sardinia, an ancient type of singing exists in which men sing in quartets and quintets using tight harmonies and producing a strange nasal, guttural sound. This type of singing flourished on Sardinia and other islands that were physically and culturally separated from the European mainland. In southern Spain, the roots of flamenco music evolved from many sources, and may have been brought there by gypsies arriving as early as the fifteenth century. At some point, Arabic music strongly influenced flamenco, and today much of the music of Spain has a strong Middle Eastern flavor. Flamenco songs often express pain, and the melodies and dances come across with passion and emotion. In Norway, where fiddling is prevalent, folk songs have a strong, constant beat, but the rhythms can be extremely difficult to follow. Although their instruments and customs may be similar, other

Name _____ Date _____ Class _____

Lesson 4

Scandinavians and even Norwegians from another area might not be able to dance to a complex folk song from a specific region.

The bagpipe is one of the earliest instruments to emerge from Europe. It is still found today in a wide range of countries. The bag itself is usually made from an animal's stomach lining and hollow sticks with finger holes are connected to the bag. Most bagpipes produce a steady note called a drone, which serves as the base note for the melody that is played on another pipe. Although the most famous bagpipes are from Scotland and Ireland, pipes also exist in Bulgaria, Greece, Italy, France, Spain, and other European countries.

Celtic music covers a wide geographic area including Wales, Scotland, Ireland, parts of Spain and France, and other areas. There is a common range of instruments shared in the region including bagpipes, harp, and fiddle, but since there are so many different styles of music in these areas, it is hard to describe exactly what makes Celtic music "Celtic."

Above all, it is probably the people's deep emotions and shared heritage that date back to when the ancient Celts settled these lands.

The European folk music of today includes a rich variety of styles within a partially shared cultural heritage. Historical factors like the spread of Christianity, classical music, political reunification, a common currency, and modern transportation and media have tended to culturally unite the continent. Despite these shared values, however, geographical features have for thousands of years isolated one region from another. Not surprisingly, the effects of geography and history are still very clearly heard in the music traditions of Europe.

Musician playing bagpipes

Folk Scat, a Bulgarian folk group, fuses traditional Bulgarian music with jazz scat singing—a creative mix.

World Music: A Cultural Legacy   33

Name _____ Date _____ Class _____

Lesson 4

Europe
Student Worksheet

DIRECTIONS: Read about the music of Europe on pages 31–33. Then using the essay and, if necessary, your geography text as references, answer the following questions in the spaces provided.

1. Which type of European music has been heavily influenced by the Middle East?

   _____

2. Name two musical instruments that are commonly found in the music of Scotland and Ireland.

   _____

   _____

3. What are two reasons why customs and music traditions are so different from one country to another in Europe?

   _____

   _____

   _____

   _____

   _____

   _____

4. Name two instruments that are native to continental Europe.

   _____

   _____

   _____

5. Name two instruments that were developed in Europe based on earlier instruments from other lands.

   _____

   _____

   _____

World Music: A Cultural Legacy

Name _____ Date _____ Class _____

Lesson 4

Music of Europe

DIRECTIONS: As you listen to the music of Europe on Disc One, Tracks 13-19 (Cassette 1, Side A), answer the questions that follow in the spaces provided.

TRACK 13 SPANISH FUSION

Song "Fiestas en Nuevo México"
© ℗ 1986, 1990, Music of the World
By: Carlos Lomas

This modern composition incorporates flamenco guitar, hand claps *(palmas)*, bass, and drums. The effect is captivating and immediately appealing.

1. Notice the brief periods of silence whenever the guitar is the only instrument playing. What type of effect does this have on the listener?

   _____

   _____

   _____

TRACK 14 SWEDEN

Song "Frog Tune"
© ℗ 1996, Music of the World
By: Swedish Sax Septet

Dark and mysterious, this piece might make you feel like looking over your shoulder. The alto sax solo adds to your heightened imagination.

1. What is something musically unusual that you notice about this song?

   _____

   _____

2. List some words you would use to describe the way this song makes you feel.

   _____

   _____

   _____

World Music: A Cultural Legacy   **35**

Name _____ Date _____ Class _____

Lesson 4

TRACK 15 — ROMANIA

Song: "Hora: ca din caval"
© ℗ 1996, Music of the World
By: Musicians from the village of Marsa, Giurgiu County

In this piece the violinist gets a unique sound by tying a single horse hair, covered with rosin, to the low (G) string of the violin. The musician is not bowing the violin. The sounds and melody are produced by pulling down on the horse hair with two fingers.

1. If you try to imagine the musicians in this song, do you think of city people or country people? Explain your answer.

   _____
   _____
   _____

2. List some words to describe the mood of this song.

   _____
   _____
   _____

TRACK 16 — THE BRITISH ISLES

Song: "The Flight"
© ℗ 1997, Alula Records
By: Johnny Cunningham

In this original Irish composition, the fiddle and accordion play in such a fast tempo that it is hard to sit still.

1. Aside from the bagpipe and fiddle, what other string instrument do you hear that gives the song a more modern sound?

   _____
   _____
   _____

World Music: A Cultural Legacy

Name _____ Date _____ Class _____

Lesson 4

TRACK 17 BRITTANY

Song "Ar Skrilhed"
Ⓒ 1989, Music of the World;
Ⓟ 1996, Music of the World
By: Paul Huellou

This piece is based on a traditional Celtic-influenced song from Brittany, in northwestern France.

1. This type of song from Brittany contains many short verses that make up a very long story. What is unique about the music structure that allows the singer to relate the whole tale in just a few minutes?

_____

_____

TRACK 18 BULGARIA

Song "Ianinku"
Ⓒ Ⓟ 1996, Music of the World
By: Folk Scat

This song is about Ianinku, a young woman whose intense beauty causes unrest among her family members. The five singers' harmonies and rhythmic elements evoke a modern jazz sound, but the main melody line is unmistakably Bulgarian.

1. This song is performed mostly with voices, but there are also a few musical instruments present. Name the instruments.

_____

_____

TRACK 19 SICILY

Song "Danse A Trois"
Ⓒ Ⓟ 1993, Music of the World
By: Enzo Rao

This composition was inspired by a Sicilian folk dance and is structured by the instruments, which divide the rhythm.

1. Arrange the following instruments in the order in which they appear in the song: violin, tambourine, bass, drums, and saxophone.

_____

World Music: A Cultural Legacy   37

Name _____ Date _____ Class _____

Lesson 4

Exploring Regional Music
Student Activity 4-A

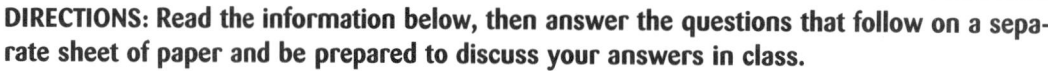

DIRECTIONS: Read the information below, then answer the questions that follow on a separate sheet of paper and be prepared to discuss your answers in class.

THE GYPSIES AND EASTERN EUROPEAN FOLK MUSIC

When we think of European music, our most familiar sound images may be of French accordions or Spanish flamenco guitars. An entirely different world of sound exists in the Eastern European countries, however.

The Gypsies are descendants of the Rom people, wandering nomads who, it is believed, originated in northern India and spread throughout Europe. The millions of Gypsies that are scattered throughout the world are often musicians, but there is no central type of music common to all of them. A high concentration of performing musicians resides in the Eastern European countries, especially in Romania and Hungary. Gypsies are respected for being very talented when it comes to making music, and it may be that performing music also suits their wandering lifestyle. Professional musicians do not work every day, but when they perform at special ceremonies they are usually paid quite well. Gypsy musicians are regularly hired to perform at social events such as weddings, funerals, and other festivities, including when soldiers go off to the army around the end of every year.

Songs and playing techniques are passed down from generation to generation, and are usually not written down. From an early age children often play along with their parents and family members. In this way they grow up with the music in their blood. Traditional string instruments such as violin, cello, and bass fiddle are played in unconventional ways using scales and rhythms that are not generally performed in Western Europe. Other typical instruments from the region include the *cimbalom* (hammered dulcimer), *cobza* (lute), accordion, and *gardon* (a type of cello played by hitting the strings with a stick).

In Transylvania you can still find traditional Sunday afternoon gatherings where villagers come to dance for hours in the streets. Throughout Romania, wedding celebrations continue into the wee hours of the morning, with non-stop music and dancing. Through all of life's major passages—birth, engagement, marriage, and death—music has a major role to play in the daily lives of the people of Eastern Europe.

An example of Romanian Gypsy music can be heard on Glencoe's "World Music: A Cultural Legacy" audio program—Disc One, Track 15 (Cassette 1, Side A).

QUESTIONS TO CONSIDER

1. Among the Gypsies, live music and dancing are a required part of almost all social activities, and children learn the music by playing with their parents. Is music performed and learned this way in your community? Why or why not?

2. What types of social activities require live music in your community?

Name _____ Date _____ Class _____

Lesson 4

Exploring Regional Music
Student Activity 4-B

DIRECTIONS: Read the information below, then answer the questions that follow on a separate sheet of paper and be prepared to discuss your answers in class.

CELTIC MUSIC

Celtic music and culture crosses many political borders. Ireland, Wales, England, Scotland, France, and Spain all share a Celtic heritage that stretches back many years. The recent rebirth of Celtic music was triggered by the folk music revival, which took place in the United States and Europe in the 1960s. Folk groups and associations in Ireland, England, and France began to investigate their ethnic roots more thoroughly, and they uncovered a rich and exciting Celtic heritage.

One would expect that Celtic music would be prominent in the British Isles, but it is interesting to see and hear Celtic influences across the English Channel in Brittany (the northwest region of France), and all the way down to Asturias and Galicia in northwest Spain. The Celts fled to Brittany in the fifth and sixth centuries after the Anglo-Saxon invasion of Britain. The Breton language is still widely spoken there, and song and dance traditions are quite different from those in the rest of France. On the north Atlantic coast of Spain, bagpipes and accordions play songs that remind us of traditional Irish or Scottish music. Spanish bagpipe schools have come into prominence and even the *hurdy-gurdy* (a drone instrument bowed by means of a rotating wheel) has been revived.

There are a variety of Celtic instruments shared throughout the region. Bagpipes are made in different shapes and sizes. They are played by blowing or pumping air into a bag usually made from an animal's stomach. Flute-like pipes are attached to the bag and, as air escapes, the musician plays a melody on the holes of the pipe. The tin whistle is the most common flute in the region. It is made of metal and usually has six holes. Accordions come in the button variety and also with keys on the right-hand side. A popular percussion instrument is the bodhran, a large frame drum played with a small double-headed stick. Many dance tunes are either "jigs" played in 6/8 time or "reels" played in 4/4 time. Dancing is a very important part of music in the Celtic tradition, and all-night dance parties take place in pubs and community halls in towns across the region.

An example of Celtic music from Ireland can be heard on Glencoe's "World Music: A Cultural Legacy" audio program—Disc One, Track 16 (Cassette 1, Side A). Track 17 is a Celtic song from Brittany.

QUESTIONS TO CONSIDER

1. The influence of Celtic music can be found far away from where it originated. Using an atlas, measure the approximate distance from the southern coast of Ireland to the northern coast of Spain. How do you think Celtic influences reached Spain?

2. Of all the instruments mentioned above, which one do you think is used most in other areas around the world? What are some other countries that use this instrument?

World Music: A Cultural Legacy

Name _____ Date _____ Class _____

Lesson 5

Music of Russia

DIRECTIONS: Read the information below, and use it to complete the Lesson 5 Student Worksheet.

The music of Russia is steeped in age-old traditions. Solo singing is common among herders, string instruments mix with accordions in the folk music of farming communities, and a strong legacy of choral music is found in cities and towns throughout the region. Despite the wide variety of ethnic groups and customs in Russia, several broadly similar patterns exist, allowing for a unification of the population through music.

Early Sacred Music

Russian liturgical music has a long history that spans more than a thousand years. Instrumental music was strictly forbidden in churches and during religious services; only vocal music was allowed. Ancient Byzantine choral melodies were sung in Russia up until the seventeenth century. These early pieces are difficult to recreate today, however, because they were written in a special type of notation that only showed the general shape of the melody, not the exact notes. Unlike choruses today who refer to sheet music for each note of the songs they sing, singers of long ago committed entire songs to memory. Today Russian Orthodox choral music still has an important place in religious ceremonies and in churches throughout the nation.

Vocal Choruses

There is something about a large group of people singing together that reaches deeply into the hearts of human beings. Russia's choral music brings about strong emotions in both the performer and the listener. Songs often begin with a solo voice, which is later joined by others in unison. After a period of singing in unison, the singers break into different parts of harmony.

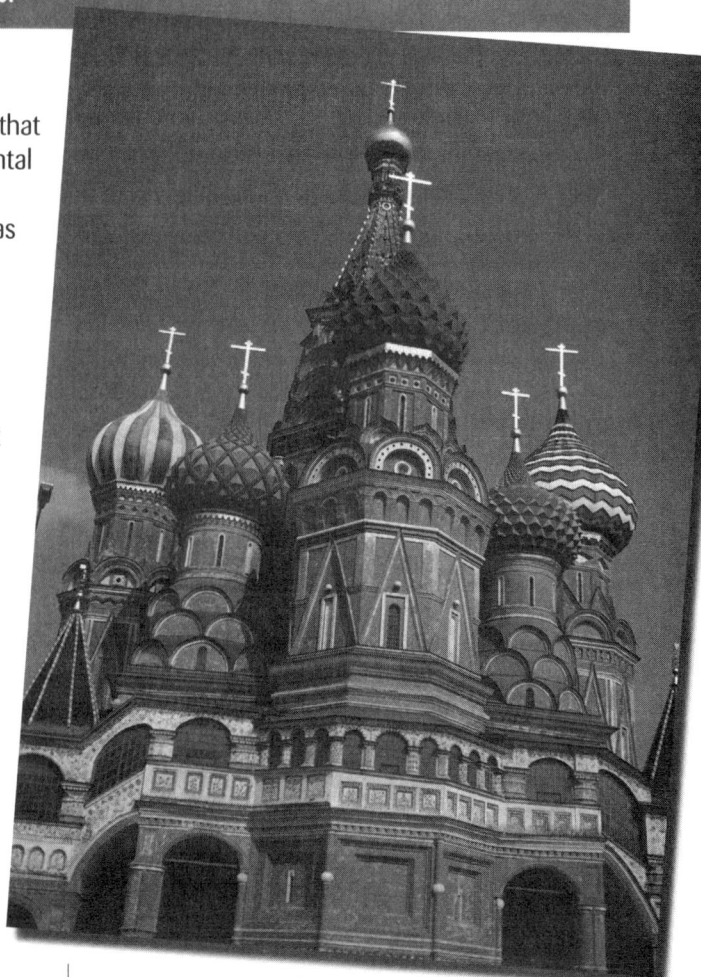

St. Basil's Cathedral in Moscow is a Russian Orthodox church.

40   World Music: A Cultural Legacy

Lesson 5

Throughout Russia there are folk choruses that sing in complex harmonies for social events and also for religious services in the Eastern Orthodox Church. Russian choral singing is characterized by changes in density, or dynamic range. The music can begin in soft tones and then suddenly become very loud, or a single voice might be immediately followed by the overwhelming power of an entire choir singing together.

Music plays a powerful role in the way it can bind communities together. The practice and hard work required to sing complex vocal harmonies symbolically and literally represents one's ability to live in harmony within a community. Only through many years of practicing together can a group of singers master the unwritten rules of blending their voices.

Folk Music

Folk music in Russia is performed by a wide variety of ethnic groups in the region. Each small group has its own traditions, customs, and ways of life. These groups' lifestyles are reflected in folk songs, which are handed down through oral tradition from one generation to the next. Some traditional songs are believed to have magical powers that protect people from evil spirits. Love songs sometimes compare human yearnings to caged birds, whose hearts cannot sing until they are set free. Other songs are connected to the natural environment, and are used for planting and harvesting crops, and to give rise to the astronomical cycles that divide the year into light and dark seasons. At weddings, guests are often entertained by storytellers who chant or sing epic tales, some of which may contain thousands of verses.

Among Russians and other Slavic peoples, an important musical form used especially at weddings and funerals is the lament. For many centuries, village brides have sung laments during the few days before a wedding, since at this time, they get ready to leave their homes to move in with their new husband's family. Laments are also used to aid in the

Russian street performers on Arbat Street in Moscow.

process of grieving when a loved one passes away. These songs are characterized by loud wailing. They do not have a strong rhythmic structure. The singing sounds somewhat like howling, and contains sliding notes and vocal flutters similar to yodeling.

There is a type of Russian folk song called *chastushka,* which consists of short verses sung, composed, and improvised mostly by girls. This type of singing became popular in the late 1800s when rural villagers migrated to larger towns and cities to look for work. Many of these songs speak about love and personal relationships, but lyrics also reflect work and political issues. The *chastushka* was once a favorite music style promoted by the government. Although government influence over the population has diminished in recent years, the *chastushka* is still heard in Russia.

World Music: A Cultural Legacy

Lesson 5

Herding Music and Throat Singing

The vast grasslands of southern Siberia are home to nomadic and semi-nomadic people who herd mainly sheep, cattle, camels, or yaks. These herders share a rich oral music tradition, with special emphasis on solo singing, storytelling, and string music.

The most characteristic ethnic music from this region comes from Tuva, a tiny autonomous republic near the Russian border with Mongolia. The Tuvans' music is a strange and unusual type of singing called throat singing, or overtone singing. By contracting and expanding muscles in the throat, larynx, tongue, and jaw, one singer can produce two notes simultaneously by selectively bringing out the harmonics (overtones) naturally present in the human voice. In this way, one person can sing both melody and accompaniment; a good form of companionship and entertainment for those lonely nomadic journeys with their herds. In this ancient style of singing, the high, whistling sound is most often meant to imitate the sound of birds, horses, or wind whistling through the grass and trees. Throat singing is also common with herders in neighboring Outer Mongolia.

Tuvans share with Mongolians and other Asian herding peoples a family of instruments called horsehead fiddles, which may be the ancient ancestors of the European violin. In these remote areas, the horse is often the only means of transport and as such commands great respect. Horsehead fiddles are covered with horsehide. The strings are made from horse gut and the bow is made of horsehair. At the end of the fiddle's neck, a carved wooden horse head is attached. Many of the songs and melodies played on these instruments relate stories about horses and about traveling.

Russian Folk Instruments

There is a rich variety of folk instruments in Russia. The most popular one is the balalaika, which probably appeared in Russia during the seventeenth century. It was common to hear the balalaika in the courts of the czar. The balalaika is also a part of everyday life in small villages throughout the region. This national instrument of Russia has a triangular wooden body, three strings, and a long neck. It ranges in size and tone from soprano to bass. Another Russian instrument, the *rojok*, is a trumpet carved from a single piece of wood, usually an apple tree. For hundreds of years, this instrument has been the favorite of shepherds and cowherds, who use it to call and herd their animals. *Lojki* are wooden spoons used as percussion instruments and played especially at weddings and other village celebrations. The *bandoura* is a large, short-necked lute with an almost circular face and up to 30 strings. Playing techniques incorporate strumming and individual fingering of the strings.

Nomadic herders in Siberia

Lesson 5

Accordions are very common and well loved in Russia. The *livenskaya* accordion produces different notes depending on whether air is squeezed into or pulled out of the bellows. The *bayan* accordion has 52 melody keys for the right hand and 100 bass notes and chords for the left hand.

Classical and Modern Music

Russia today boasts great symphony orchestras and some of the finest classical musicians in the world. The most famous Russian classical composer was Peter Tchaikovsky, whose most recognizable compositions are *The Nutcracker Suite* and his ballets, *Swan Lake* and *Sleeping Beauty*. Russia also produced Mikhail Baryshnikov, a ballet dancer who settled in the United States and delighted audiences with a grace and style rarely seen before.

Rock music is quite popular in Russia, especially in the large cities of Moscow and St. Petersburg, where original compositions as well as cover tunes of Western rock stars are regularly heard in the clubs. In the 1970s and 1980s, rock music was an important vehicle for protesting the Soviet Communist regime. It had a strong effect in uniting young people for a single cause. In recent years, jazz has also seen a rise in popularity, and Russian jazz musicians regularly perform and tour on the international circuits.

Because of the cultural diversity in Russia, and despite the uniformity promoted by the government of the former Soviet Union, this region offers a wide range of music and artistic expression.

A traditional balalaika ensemble

World Music: A Cultural Legacy   43

Name _____ Date _____ Class _____

Lesson 5
Russia
Student Worksheet

DIRECTIONS: Read about the music of Russia on pages 40–43. Then using the essay and, if necessary, your geography text as references, answer the following questions in the spaces provided.

1. Name and describe four types of Russian music that have no equivalent in the United States and Canada. Explain the purposes these types of music serve in Russian tradition.

   a) _____

   b) _____

   c) _____

   d) _____

2. Before reading this essay, if you had been asked what types of instruments and music were played in Russia, what would you have answered?

3. What are the most surprising and interesting things you learned from this essay? Explain.

44   World Music: A Cultural Legacy

Name _____ Date _____ Class _____

Lesson 5

Music of Russia

DIRECTIONS: As you listen to the music of Russia on Disc One, Tracks 20-23 (Cassette 1, Side B), answer the questions that follow in the spaces provided.

TRACK 20 RUSSIA

Song "Kalinka"
© ℗ 1995, ARC Music Productions Int.
By: The Stars of St. Petersburg

This is a popular Russian tune played with unusual sensitivity. The instruments include bass, guitar, accordion, tambourine, and balalaika.

1. This song goes through several stages of slow and then fast playing. What effect does this have on you as a listener? How do you feel when the music suddenly slows down after a very fast section?

   _____
   _____
   _____

TRACK 21 TUVA

Song "Taraan Taraam Dazir Sholde"
© ℗ 1998, Amiata Records
By: Igor Koshkendey

After the first sung verse, the "throat singing" is heard as a sharp whistling sound. Notice that the singing moves up and down a scale while the bottom note stays constant.

1. Are the singer and string instruments playing the same melody?

   _____
   _____

2. At which part of the song do the string players play a single drone note?

   _____
   _____

World Music: A Cultural Legacy **45**

Name _____ Date _____ Class _____

Lesson 5

TRACK 22 — RUSSIAN CHORAL MUSIC

Song: "Vysbranny Voyevodiye"
© ℗ 1996, ARC Music Productions Int.
By: Tolstiakov

This is a recording of nineteenth-century liturgical music from Russia.

1. Without understanding the words, what kind of mood does this song communicate to the listener? List a few words you would use to describe the feeling of this song.

   _____
   _____
   _____
   _____
   _____
   _____

TRACK 23 — RUSSIAN POLKA

Song: "Polka"
© ℗ 1998, ARC Music Productions Int.
By: Olga Mischula and Kermash

This Russian dance tune has a tempo that accelerates over a period of time, with the song ending in a frenzy. Imagine how fast you would have to be dancing to this song!

1. There are only three instruments playing in this song. One is a string instrument called a dulcimer, played with small wooden hammers. What are the other two instruments?

   _____
   _____
   _____
   _____
   _____

World Music: A Cultural Legacy

Name _____ Date _____ Class _____

Lesson 5

Exploring Regional Music
Student Activity 5

DIRECTIONS: Read the information below, then answer the questions that follow on a separate sheet of paper and be prepared to discuss your answers in class.

TUVAN THROAT SINGING

Tuva is a small independent Russian republic that lies within a ring of mountains where southern Siberia meets Outer Mongolia. A large group of nomadic herders founded the country in 1921. The primary means of transport of these herders, even today, is the horse. This is a region where the great conqueror Genghis Khan once came to recruit his warrior horsemen. Throughout Tuva, southern Siberia, and Mongolia, nomadic shepherds tell stories and play interesting string instruments, including the horsehead fiddle. The most characteristic music of the region, however, is an incredibly unusual type of singing known as *khoomei*, commonly referred to in the West as "throat singing."

Some people say that throat singing was developed by shepherds who, while tending to their flocks, tried to sing two or more notes at once. The "notes" are actually called overtones. They can be produced in the human throat cavity by anyone who practices long and hard enough. This distinctive singing style has two components—a constant vowel sound that is produced deep in the throat and a whistling sound that moves up and down a scale. Melodies are created using the notes of the whistle tones while the drone of the lower tone remains constant. The whistle tones are produced by tightening and loosening one's throat, lip, jaw, and cheek muscles. The tighter the muscles are squeezed, the higher the pitch of the sounds.

In Tuva there are three basic styles of throat singing—one imitates soft summer breezes and bird songs, another resembles the howling of harsh winter winds, and yet another evokes the sound of the wind as it swirls through grasslands and around craggy mountains and large rocks. In traditional Tuvan society throat singing was reserved for adult males who recounted stories of life and adventure on the grasslands. In recent times, however, females, children, and even outsiders have begun to enjoy throat singing as a form of fun and recreation. There are throat singing competitions held every year in Tuva, and people from all over the world come to compete in these contests and share their songs.

An example of Tuvan throat singing can be heard on Glencoe's "World Music: A Cultural Legacy" audio program–Disc One, Track 21 (Cassette 1, Side B).

QUESTIONS TO CONSIDER

1. Why do you think nomadic shepherds have such a strong solo vocal tradition and do not usually play other instruments in groups?
2. What do you think is unique about the lifestyle of shepherds that may have produced a way of singing more than one note at the same time?
3. Do you think throat singing has a ceremonial significance or is it just used as entertainment? Explain your answer.

World Music: A Cultural Legacy

Name _____ Date _____ Class _____

Lesson 6
Music of North Africa, Southwest Asia, and Central Asia

DIRECTIONS: Read the information below, and use it to complete the Lesson 6 Student Worksheet.

The region of North Africa, Southwest Asia (commonly known as the Middle East), and Central Asia is the home of many ethnic, religious, and linguistic groups. The dominant cultures and languages are Arabic (variations of which are spoken throughout the Middle East), Persian (Farsi is the language, as in Iran), and Turkish (Turkey). The region also includes a wide range of ethnic minorities including Berbers, Kurds, and others. Throughout the area there are shared values evident in music and culture, but with the intermingling of local traditions, and as a result of influences from Central Asia, Europe, and India, there is also great variety in the cultural expressions of the region.

Islam: One Faith, Many Cultures

The main force of cultural unity in this region is the religion and way of life known as Islam. In A.D. 622 the prophet Mohammad made a celebrated flight from his hometown of Makkah (now in Saudi Arabia) to nearby Madinah. Within a century, Islam became one of the dominant religions of the world. It became a basis for inspiration in music, fine arts, agriculture, medicine, philosophy, mathematics, and other forms of social and spiritual growth. In addition to shared religious values, political power also helped create cultural unity. For a long period of time, Arabs (A.D. 750-1250), and later Turks (A.D. 1325-1918) ruled vast regions throughout Southwest Asia. They used a shared written language, Arabic, to write about philosophy, science, and music. Even today, ancient texts influence music theory and practice throughout this region.

Music in Southwest Asia and North Africa

Traditional music in Southwest Asia and North Africa can be divided into three closely related branches: Arab, Persian, and Turkish. They are all

This nineteenth-century Turkish Islamic decorative tile bears the inscription "Allah is Great."

48 World Music: A Cultural Legacy

Name _____ Date _____ Class _____

Lesson 6

Hassan Hakmoun plays traditional Moroccan Gnawa music, a type of music that is meant to appeal to the spiritual world. Hakmoun plays the *sintir*, a three-stringed bass lute.

Melody

Each melody is based on a melodic mode known in the Arab countries and Turkey as *maqam (makam)*, and in the Persian system as *dastgah*. There are hundreds of these modes, and to be considered a good musician, you must master at least 20 of them. Unlike the 12-tone scale we use in the West, the tones of a *maqam* are selected from a scale of 17 or more pitches. This means that musicians are able to perform and sing notes that fall between the black and white notes on a piano. These pitches, called semitones or microtones, are an important identifying feature of Southwest Asian and North African music, and as we will learn later in this program, they are found in other important music cultures around the world. Because of this and other factors, music from this region may be related in structure and form, but each branch has retained and advanced a unique musical identity.

Today in the Arab world, large orchestras combining traditional instruments of the region and Western classical instruments are common. There is also a strong tradition based on solo or small ensemble performances in which the human voice plays an important role. As with music in India and the Far East, all members in a group play the same basic melody, but individual musicians have the freedom to embellish and vary the main notes according to their own tastes and abilities. In addition to the main melody lines of a composition, there is also much freedom given to improvisation. At certain points in a piece, for example, musicians are allowed to perform solos by improvising around standard melodic ideas, but using only the notes of the mode (or scale) of that particular piece.

Turkish musician Bayram Bilge Toker is known as a masterful *saz (baglama)* player.

World Music: A Cultural Legacy

Lesson 6

considered much more expressive than music in the West. On the other hand, the music in this region generally does not utilize harmony, or the playing of several notes together as chords.

Rhythm

Rhythm is highly developed in Southwest Asian (Middle Eastern) and North African music, and is built on a complex system of cycles that incorporate strong and weak beats. The beats are often grouped in clusters, which are strung together to create a full cycle. In Western music for example, a common rhythm is an eight-beat pattern, and in most cases, the numbers are counted 1 through 8 with the strong beat as 1 and the weak beats as 2 through 7. In the music of Southwest Asia and North Africa, however, these same eight beats could be grouped as 3 + 3 + 2 (with the first note of each group counted as a strong beat); or maybe 4 + 4 (with 2 strong beats); or 2 + 4 + 2 (3 strong beats), and so on. Such uneven patterns lend an exciting flavor to the rhythm, and keep it propelling forward in combination with the melody lines.

Musical Instruments

With the great variety of musical styles in this region, it is not surprising that there is an equally great diversity of musical instruments. Since playing semitones and embellishments are so important, fretless string instruments are common throughout the area. The lack of frets allows the musician to play all the subtle variations of each note by sliding a finger up or down the neck of

Aziz Herawi is a rare performer of the traditional music from the Herat valley in western Afghanistan. He plays the *dutar* and the *rebab*, which are types of lutes.

the instrument. There is also a wide range of string instruments with adjustable frets.

The most important string instrument of this region is the oud ('ud). The oud has a pear-shaped body with up to 10 strings, although 6 are common. The neck is sharply bent backward at the top of the fingerboard. The body is made of fine-grained wood, and is often beautifully inlaid with ebony or mother-of-pearl. The sound hole is usually framed by a delicately carved piece of ivory. This instrument has a very distinctive sound, and is played with a feather quill or a plectrum made of bone, horn, or wood.

Another lute, the North African *sintir (gnibri)*, is part of a family of instruments whose roots extend back to ancient Egypt. Other lutes such as the *saz* of Turkey or the *setar* of Iran have long slender necks and produce a bright, slightly buzzing sound when played. Among string instruments, zithers are also common throughout the area. Zithers are stringed instruments that usually

50 World Music: A Cultural Legacy

Lesson 6

have 30 or more strings strung over a shallow horizontal soundboard. They are played with a pick or the fingers. The *kanoon* has a bright sound since it is played with small wire picks worn on the player's fingers. The strings of the *santur*, however, are struck with small mallets producing a softer, warmer sound.

Popular drums in this region include the *dumbek (tombak)*, a metal or ceramic-bodied drum that can produce a loud, piercing sound. It has one skin head, which when struck by different combinations of fingers in different areas, can produce a wide range of tones. There is also a wide range of frame drums and tambourines in the region, as well as finger cymbals and other percussion instruments. The most important flute in the region is called *nay (nai)*. It is an end-blown flute with a very breathy tone.

In addition to the traditional music of the region, there are also some exciting modern forms of music. One of the most popular to evolve in North Africa is called *rai*, a rhythmic and very danceable music, combining traditional and modern instruments and led by a talented and versatile singer. As would be expected, Western pop and rock have influenced the younger generation and help bring about new fusions of music. As new forms of music continue to evolve in the region, there will probably always be a strong social identity with the traditional music of its proud, ancient past.

Jalal Zolfonun, from Iran, is a master of the *setar*.

Hamsa el Din, a musician from Sudan, plays the oud.

World Music: A Cultural Legacy 51

Name _____ Date _____ Class _____

Lesson 6

North Africa, Southwest Asia, and Central Asia
Student Worksheet

DIRECTIONS: Read about the music of North Africa, Southwest Asia, and Central Asia on pages 48–51. Then using the essay and, if necessary, your geography text as references, answer the following questions in the spaces provided.

1. What language is spoken in Iran?

   _____

2. Describe at least two distinguishing features of the music of North Africa, Southwest Asia, and Central Asia.

   _____

   _____

   _____

   _____

   _____

   _____

   _____

3. The music of Spain was influenced strongly by the music of North Africa and Southwest Asia. Look at a map of the region and list below the African country that is physically closest to Spain.

   _____

   _____

4. The oud is the most common string instrument in the region. Which popular musical instrument of today do you think is a direct descendant of the oud?

   _____

   _____

   _____

52 World Music: A Cultural Legacy

Name _____ Date _____ Class _____

Lesson 6

Music of North Africa, Southwest Asia, and Central Asia

DIRECTIONS: As you listen to the music of North Africa, Southwest Asia, and Central Asia on Disc One, Tracks 24-29 (Cassette 1, Side B), answer the questions that follow in the spaces provided.

TRACK 24 MOROCCO

Song "Wa yay yay Saadiya"
ⓒ 1989, World Music Institute;
ⓟ 1995, Music of the World
By: Hassan Hakmoun

This is a traditional song used in religious ceremonies. The main instrument is the *sintir*, a three-stringed, skin-faced lute.

1. Listen to the entire song. The bass-like instrument you hear is the *sintir*. What other sounds can you identify, and what is producing them?

_____

_____

_____

TRACK 25 ISRAEL

Song "Trance"
ⓒ 1998, Amiata Records; ⓟ 1998
Amiata Records & Najema Music
By: Yair Dalal and the Al Ol Ensemble

This is a mixture of Jewish and Arabic music, based on a Turkish folk tune in which the clarinet improvisation is dominant.

1. We know that in the music of North Africa and Southwest Asia there are generally no chords. While the clarinet is playing his solo, all the other instruments are playing a drone of a single note. In your own words, what kind of effect does this have on the music and on the listener?

_____

_____

_____

_____

World Music: A Cultural Legacy   53

Name _____ Date _____ Class _____

Lesson 6

TRACK 26 | AFGHANISTAN

Song: "Aushari-Naghmaha-ye Logari"
© 1990, World Music Institute;
℗ 1996, Music of the World
By: Aziz Herawi Ensemble

This is a celebrated dance called *Aushari*, popular in the Herati region of Afghanistan.

1. Judging by the sound coming from the main string instrument, do you think it is played with the fingers or with some sort of pick or plectrum?

   _____
   _____
   _____
   _____

TRACK 27 | IRAN

Song: "Neyriz"
© ℗ 1999, Music of the World
By: Jalal and Soheil Zolfonun

Neyriz is a traditional song from Iran.

1. How many instruments do you hear playing?

   _____

2. Notice that there are short passages of silence in this piece. Describe, in your own words, the effect this silence has on the listener and on the song.

   _____
   _____
   _____
   _____
   _____
   _____

World Music: A Cultural Legacy

Name _____ Date _____ Class _____

Lesson 6

TRACK 28 | ARMENIA

Song "Tamzara"
 1995, American Recording Productions
By: The Ara Topouzian Ensemble

This song is a modern variation of a traditional dance melody from Armenia.

1. A common rhythm in Western music has eight beats. This song has a different number of beats, however. If you lightly tap the beat in steady intervals, occasionally one of your taps will "miss" the beat. How many beats do you think this song has?

   _____

2. At the end of the song, after all the instruments finish playing the song together, what does the lone clarinet do?

   _____

   _____

TRACK 29 | TURKEY

Song "Kurdili Hicazkar Fasli"
 1992, Music of the World
By: Necdet Yasar Ensemble

This is a Turkish musical form called *fasil*. The piece itself is more than 20 minutes long, and features a singer and a full orchestra.

1. As soon as the singer begins, do the other instruments play different notes or the same notes as the singer?

   _____

   _____

2. Is there any harmony in this piece or do all instruments basically play the same melody in unison?

   _____

   _____

World Music: A Cultural Legacy 55

Name _____ Date _____ Class _____

Exploring Regional Music
Student Activity 6

DIRECTIONS: Read the information below, then answer the questions that follow on a separate sheet of paper and be prepared to discuss your answers in class.

THE GNAWA, MUSICAL HEALERS FROM MOROCCO

Have you ever noticed how certain types of music make you feel happy or sad, sleepy or energetic? Music no doubt produces strong effects on people, and in certain cultures all over the globe it is used as a tool for healing.

The Gnawa are a traditional people, descendants of enslaved persons originally brought across the Sahara by the Arabs. Although the Gnawa live throughout Morocco, they are mostly concentrated around the area of Marrakech. Each afternoon in the huge city square, groups of Gnawa perform acrobatic dances to the accompaniment of live music. The sound of the drums not only entertains audiences, but the performances are thought to bring to life any spirits that may have settled in the neighborhood.

For most Gnawa, the role of entertainer is secondary to their more important (and secret) role as musical healers in the spirit world. Most Gnawa ceremonies, or *derdeba*, are held to soothe spirits, both good and evil, that inhabit a certain person or place. Gnawa are often called in to treat victims of physical problems, snake and scorpion bites, and also mental illnesses. Healing ceremonies can last for many hours—sometimes throughout an entire day and night! The Gnawa believe that these ceremonies very often result in the spirit being expelled from the person or place in question. In addition to purging evil spirits that may have caused illness, infertility, or other afflictions, *derdebas* are also carried out to extend a happy relationship with a good spirit that has brought wealth, happiness, or another blessing to a person.

The main instrument of the Gnawa is the *sintir,* a type of long-necked lute that is similar to string instruments found in other parts of Africa. The *sintir,* with its wooden body and face covered in animal skin, produces a deep bass tone. It is plucked and slapped in a percussive manner, and it is usually accompanied by large metal clappers or castanets called *qaraqeb,* which beat out a steady, pulsating rhythm. These instruments, along with the human voice, form the basis for the trance-like healing music of Morocco.

An example of Gnawa healing music can be heard on Glencoe's "World Music: A Cultural Legacy" audio program—Disc One, Track 24 (Cassette 1, Side B).

QUESTIONS TO CONSIDER

1. In a proper environment, and given a certain state of mind, do you believe that music and sound can be effective in curing people of certain afflictions? Why or why not?

2. Can you think of any other cultures, including your own, in which music is an important part of healing ceremonies? Explain your answer.

Name _____ Date _____ Class _____

Lesson 7
Music of Africa South of the Sahara

DIRECTIONS: Read the information below, and use it to complete the Lesson 7 Student Worksheet.

More so than in other cultures around the world, music is an essential part of everyday life in Africa. Music here is fundamentally rhythm-based, even when it is played on melodic instruments. In addition to serving as entertainment, music plays an important role in religious rituals, provides motivation for manual labor, teaches children through fables, empowers dance ceremonies, and records historical events and genealogy. Almost every aspect of African life has an accompanying musical component.

Africa is an enormous continent with many countries and almost 1,000 languages and dialects. Each ethnic group has its own style of music. Although there are major similarities in the structure and performance of music throughout the region, there are also many differences in music styles and instruments from one culture group to another. Even in modern times, many of these culture groups maintain their individual music, language, customs, and social behavior. This is what makes Africa such a unique and diverse place.

Musical Complexity

Music in Africa can be extremely complex, both in melody and rhythm. It is not uncommon for an accomplished musician to play two or three melodies using different combinations of fingers on both hands, while perhaps even singing a fourth melody at the same time. In drumming, each player may have a different rhythm to play, and the accents (hard and soft beats) of these parts often fall in different places. This layering and interlocking of two or more rhythms at the same time is called *polyrhythm*. Africa reigns supreme in the variety and complexity of the polyrhythms it contributes to the world of music.

Dance

Throughout Africa, percussion instruments such as drums, rattles, and bells are a vital part of every dance ensemble. Dance is a fundamental

James Makubuya belongs to the Baganda people of the ancient Ugandan kingdom. His ensemble plays traditional East African instruments.

World Music: A Cultural Legacy   **57**

Lesson 7

Senegalese musician Djimo Kouyate, here playing a *kora*, comes from a long line of griots.

as he or she plays, giving musical signals to the accompanying musicians so they can keep their place in the song. With drumming troupes, the improvisation sometimes passes from one player to another, adding even more variation and excitement to the music. Men and boys usually play drums and melodic instruments, while women and girls play percussion instruments such as rattles and scrapers. In dance music, women often layer precise hand clapping parts on top of the drumming, making the polyrhythms even more complex. Women are respected for their singing abilities, and often perform for festive events and special ceremonies. Even in singing, there is improvisation in Africa. An accomplished improviser will take special note of the people present in the audience, and oftentimes compose a line or a verse about them right on the spot.

part of African society, and children are immersed in a dance environment from a very early age. It is important to note that dance plays a much more prominent role in African music events than it does in the West. In our culture, one is expected to be quiet and still at a funeral, whereas in Africa, dance is commonplace at funerals, and is used as a way to express sadness and grief. At a performance or public concert, instead of clapping, Africans may come to the front of the circle, or jump up onto the stage and begin dancing to show their appreciation to the musicians. These are some of the ways in which music in Africa is participatory rather than performance-based.

Improvisation

Improvisation, or performing without preparation or on the spot, is also very important in African music. With both percussion and melodic instruments, the lead musician often improvises

Obo Addy presents Ghana's music culture when he performs internationally. Here he plays a large talking drum.

58   World Music: A Cultural Legacy

Name _____ Date _____ Class _____

Lesson 7

Seleshe Damessae, from Ethiopia, is a master of the *krar*. He sings in Amharic, his native language.

Music Practice and Oral History

African musicians, whether instrumentalists or singers, do not learn by reading written music or by practicing scales. As in other world cultures, the learning process takes place over time through listening and imitating. Students of music practice by regularly performing with their family members and teachers. In some cultures of Africa, people become musicians because they are born into families that have provided music for audiences for centuries. For example, the griots of West African nations such as Gambia, Senegal, and Mali pass down their talents from generation to generation. Originally, griots belonged to the royal courts and served as historians to the king. Still to this day, a griot's role is to commit to memory the family tree of all important villagers, to record historical events in song, and to transmit this information by performing at ceremonies and social events.

Drumming

An incredibly wide variety of drums are played throughout the continent of Africa. As with singing, drums are commonly heard together in groups, and they often follow a "call-and-response" style, whereby one lead drum beats out a pattern (call) and the other drums play their answer (response). This musical matrix has been prevalent in Africa since early times, and was passed on to the Western Hemisphere in the form of gospel, salsa, rock, and other types of popular music. One of the most interesting African drums is the talking drum, which is found in Nigeria, Senegal, and other areas. The wooden body of the drum is made in an hourglass shape, and skins are placed on each side and held tightly against the body with long cords. The musician places the drum under the armpit and strikes it with a curved stick, while at the same time exerting pressure on the strings that connect the skins. When the skins are stretched, the drum pitch is higher; when the skins are relaxed, the tone is lower. Coded phrases based on combinations of pitches still serve as a means of communication and, in earlier times, told stories of war, death, natural calamities, and other social issues.

Other Instruments

Among wind instruments there are vertical and transverse flutes, panpipes, ocarinas, whistles, and even nose flutes, which are blown through the nostrils instead of the mouth. In many African cultures, nose breath has a magical association, and so nose flutes are often used in religious and spiritual rituals. Reed instruments similar to clarinets and oboes are found in Africa, especially in areas where there are Islamic traditions. Trumpets and horns are also common, and can be made of animal horn, wood, or dried gourds. Their use may be ceremonial, as an alarm to warn people,

World Music: A Cultural Legacy

Lesson 7

for hunting, or as accompaniment in a large dance piece.

String instruments vary widely, and mostly consist of lyres, harps, and bowed instruments. Early East African lyres such as the Ethiopian *krar* and the Ugandan *ndongo* probably served as models for the American banjo. Harps and zithers are found throughout the continent. Two of the most well-known are the 21-string *kora* from West Africa and the *valiha*, a tubular bamboo zither from the southern island nation of Madagascar.

As you might imagine, there are many types of percussion in Africa, including gourd rattles, rasping instruments, wooden and iron bells, wooden xylophones *(balafon),* slit drums, and thumb pianos called *mbira* or *sanza*. The *mbira* is used recreationally, but the Shona people of Zimbabwe also use it in special ceremonies as a tool to contact ancestral spirits and ask them for guidance.

African Music Today

Many urban Africans ride buses, drive cars, and work in offices or factories. They usually speak several languages, including English or French. They go to parties and dance to music on recordings or played by a live band. They are familiar with the music of American and European popular musicians, but they also know the traditional music associated with their native language. Even though Western instruments such as electric guitar, bass, and synthesizer are commonly used in African pop music, traditional handmade instruments are still preferred in many areas.

Ephat Mujuru and the late Dumisani Maraire (both from Zimbabwe) brought together their skilled playing of the *mbira* on this celebrated CD.

In recent years, and through collaborations with famous Western rock artists, African pop music has reached much wider audiences throughout the world. The popular South African vocal group Ladysmith Black Mambazo was made popular in the West through their collaboration with American musician Paul Simon. Other well-known African stars have become popular through their work with European rock artists and by recording in England, France, and other nations that once held colonial rule over their homelands. As it has been for many centuries, Africa continues to influence the rest of the world with its complex, danceable, and expressive music. It will no doubt continue to influence the way music is composed and performed for many years to come.

Ladysmith Black Mambazo sings with various artists on this CD.

60   World Music: A Cultural Legacy

Name _____ Date _____ Class _____

Lesson 7
Africa South of the Sahara
Student Worksheet

DIRECTIONS: Read about the music of Africa South of the Sahara on pages 57–60. Then using the essay and, if necessary, your geography text as references, answer the following questions in the spaces provided.

1. Describe several ways African music is used for communication that do not exist in Western countries such as the United States and Canada. Be prepared to discuss your answers more fully in class.

   _____
   _____
   _____
   _____
   _____

2. Name and describe at least two uniquely African instruments that do not exist in the West.

   _____
   _____
   _____
   _____
   _____

3. Try this experiment. Start tapping slowly on a table with your left index finger. Then, in the empty space between each left-handed tap, tap two quick taps with your right index finger. Now speed up the rhythm. Based on what you have read in the essay, what have you just created?

   _____
   _____
   _____

World Music: A Cultural Legacy

Name _____ Date _____ Class _____

Music of Africa South of the Sahara

DIRECTIONS: As you listen to the music of Africa South of the Sahara on Disc Two, Tracks 1-6 (Cassette 2, Side A), answer the questions that follow in the spaces provided.

TRACK 1 NIGERIA

Song "Omoge Super"
© ℗ 1991, Music of the World
By: I.K. Dairo and His Blue Spots

This is a song about a man who wants to be married to his girlfriend. He is ready to pay a dowry for this beautiful woman.

1. One of the main instruments in this song is the accordion. How do you think the accordion became popular in Nigeria?

   _____
   _____
   _____

2. Which European nation colonized Nigeria?

   _____

TRACK 2 GAMBIA

Song "Improvisation"
© ℗ 1998, Music of the World
By: Yan Kuba Saho

This is a short excerpt of an improvised song played on the *kora*, a 21-string harp from West Africa.

1. When we think of Africa, we often call to mind drums and percussion, yet the instrument used to play this piece is a harp. How would you say the technique of playing this African harp differs from the sound of a harp you would hear in a symphony orchestra?

   _____
   _____
   _____

62   World Music: A Cultural Legacy

Name _____ Date _____ Class _____

Lesson 7

TRACK 3 — ZIMBABWE

Song: "Njari Makonde"
[c] [p] 1996, Music of the World
By: Ephat Mujuru and Dumisani Maraire

This is a traditional song from the Shona people of Zimbabwe, handed down from the ancestors, and used as a tool to communicate with the ancient spirits.

1. There are two singers performing this song. What would you say is their musical relationship? Are they singing the same melody together, or is one reinforcing the singing of the other? Describe what you hear in your own words.

   _____

   _____

   _____

   _____

TRACK 4 — GHANA

Song: "Osoleo"
[c] [p] 1990, Music of the World
By: Obo Addy and Kukrudu

This melody has been adapted from a traditional Ghanaian children's song. It combines African talking drums and vocals with a contemporary electric flavor.

1. Why might the beginning of this song sound familiar to you?

   _____

   _____

   _____

2. What characteristics point to the fact that this song is from another land, specifically Africa?

   _____

   _____

   _____

   _____

World Music: A Cultural Legacy

Name _____ Date _____ Class _____

Lesson 7

TRACK 5 UGANDA

Song "Akaliba Kange"
Ⓒ 1997, James Makubuya; ℗ 1999, Music of the World
By: James Makubuya Ensemble

In this traditional song from Uganda, a brother warns his sisters to stop playing tricks on him by hiding his dancing clothes.

1. How would you describe the structure of this song? How do the different parts of the song interact?

   _____
   _____
   _____
   _____
   _____

TRACK 6 ETHIOPIA

Song "Babure"
Ⓒ ℗ 2000, Music of the World
By: Seleshe Damessae

This song blends the traditional *krar* (an ancient lyre from Ethiopia) with a modern feeling and singing style.

1. Which parts of this piece are "catchy" and easy to remember?

   _____
   _____

2. Do you think the musician is strumming the strings with a piece of wood or with his fingers? Explain your answer.

   _____
   _____
   _____

World Music: A Cultural Legacy

Name _____ Date _____ Class _____

Lesson 7

Exploring Regional Music
Student Activity 7

DIRECTIONS: Read the information below, then answer the questions that follow on a separate sheet of paper and be prepared to discuss your answers in class.

MUSICAL HISTORIANS OF WEST AFRICA

In the West African countries of Senegal, Gambia, Mali, and outlying areas, there is a tradition of musical storytellers that dates back many centuries to the days of the great royal courts. In the Mandinka language, these people are called *jali*. The French, during their years of colonialization in the area, used the word *griot* to describe these same musicians. As keepers of the tradition, griots acted as oral historians, collecting information about people, places, and things, and then reporting back to the king on events occurring within the kingdom. These griots also composed songs for wealthy patrons, and committed to memory the family trees of important people in the community.

The most important musical instruments used by griots are the *kora* and the *balafon*. The *balafon* is a type of xylophone made with wooden keys that are lashed to a wooden frame. Small, halved gourds are hung underneath each wooden key. These halved gourds act as resonators, naturally amplifying the sounds of the keys, which are hit with cloth-covered wooden mallets. *Balafons* come in all different sizes, and they are played while sitting on the ground. Sometimes they are fitted with straps, hung around the neck, and played while standing up.

The *kora* is a 21-string harp. It has a resonating body made of a large gourd, which is covered with cowhide. A wooden pole pierces the gourd and extends outward, acting as a neck for the strings, which are fastened to it using strips of leather. Originally the strings were made of gut (animal intestines), but nowadays nylon fishing line is the preferred material. The *kora* has an unmistakably beautiful sound, and is probably the best known of all African string instruments.

Although the royal courts of the African empires are long gone, griots are still in demand in modern society. They perform for naming ceremonies, births, funerals, and other social events. The *kora* and *balafon* are used in modern African music too, and have appeared in recent years alongside electric instruments in African and Western fusion bands. This is proof that despite radical changes in social and political structure, Mandinka music and the griot tradition are still very much alive.

An example of kora *music can be heard on Glencoe's "World Music: A Cultural Legacy" audio program–Disc 2, Track 2 (Cassette 2, Side A).*

QUESTIONS TO CONSIDER

1. Make an argument for and against the spreading of news through individuals such as griots rather than through modern media such as television and newspapers. In which situations would griots and modern media be preferred? Explain your answer.
2. In many traditional societies around the world, age-old customs and music traditions still exist alongside modern values and electric music. Why do you think this is so? Why is this not as evident in the United States and Canada?

Name _____ Date _____ Class _____

Lesson 8

Music of South Asia

DIRECTIONS: Read the information below, and use it to complete the Lesson 8 Student Worksheet.

The three largest countries in South Asia are India, Bangladesh, and Pakistan. This area has one of the highest concentrations of people and one of the most diverse populations in the world. We often use the term "Indian music" to refer to the music performed and used throughout this vast area. In general terms, Indian music can be divided into four major types: 1.) religious music; 2.) folk and regional music; 3.) classical music; and 4.) modern/popular music.

Religious Music

Hinduism and Islam are the two main religions in South Asia. Both religions use music widely in their ceremonies and prayer rituals. The Hindu religion has a long tradition of music associated with ancient books known as the Vedas, which when read are chanted in a particular style. Likewise, the holy Quran of the Muslims is also read in a musical style. Modern devotional songs among the Hindu are called *bhajans*. The energetic style of popular devotional singing in Pakistan is called *qawwali*. Buddhists in South Asia and other areas routinely use chanting as a form of spiritual meditation.

Folk and Regional Music

Due to the wide variety of subcultures and languages in South Asia, the folk music varies enormously from one region to another. Much of this music is associated with particular events such as village celebrations, weddings, births, and feasts. Folk instruments include various types of bowed and plucked strings, flutes, drums, and assorted percussion.

Classical Music

Indian classical music developed from folk and religious traditions, but it is a unique system. Serious students and professional musicians must devote their entire lives to its study and practice. There are two forms of Indian

The sitar

66 World Music: A Cultural Legacy

Name _____ Date _____ Class _____

Lesson 8

Trichy Sankaran is a master percussionist from South India who specializes in playing the *mrdangam*.

Raga

A raga can be described as something between a simple scale and a complete melody. The rules of the raga system are very strict, but they also allow room for a musician to develop individual musical ideas and expressions. In Indian music, there is a basic scale of seven notes, with each note having its own name. Five of these notes have alternate forms however, so mathematically there are 72 different scales possible in South Asian music, as opposed to only a few that are used in Western classical music. In addition to so many scales, the use of semitones and pitch ornamentation lays the groundwork for a very complex and evolved melodic system.

Tala

Rhythmic structures known as talas consist of a fixed number of soft and hard beats, which in turn comprise cycles of rhythm. As with the raga (melodic) system, there is also great improvisation in the tala system. Excellent percussionists perform dazzling solos by playing "around" and not

classical music—Carnatic (South Indian) and Hindustani (North Indian). Although there are considerable stylistic differences between them, and different instruments are used in each tradition, the basic musical concept and structure are the same.

Indian music has highly developed rules regarding the use of melody and rhythm. In the West, music is largely focused on the use of harmony (two or more notes played together as a chord) and counterpoint (two or more instruments playing different melodic lines at the same time). The foundation of Indian music, however, is the interaction between melody (loosely defined as raga) and rhythm (tala). In addition, and unlike Western classical music, Indian music allows for a great amount of musical improvisation within the basic framework.

Here North Indian musicians Bikram Ghosh (left) and Tarun Bhattacharya (right) play the tabla and the *santur*.

World Music: A Cultural Legacy

Lesson 8

necessarily staying "on" the beat. Although there is a wide variety of rhythmic combinations in the Indian music system, the most common talas are of 4, 6, 7, 10, 12, 14, and 16 beats. The most common North Indian drum is called tabla, and in South India, the most common drum is called the *mrdangam*. Occasionally, when concerts are performed with both Hindustani and Carnatic musicians, the drumming exchanges between the two groups can be absolutely electrifying.

Hindustani and Carnatic Styles

There are two main branches of South Asian classical music: the Hindustani style practiced in northern India, Pakistan, and Bangladesh; and the Carnatic style of South India. Both systems share the same basic concepts of raga and tala, but their use of ornamentation, or pitch variation, may be different. Many instruments used in North Indian music have their origins in folk instruments from Persia and other northern regions. In the South, the instruments evolved from the subcontinent itself and have strong ties to India's ancient Hindu legacy. While compositions in the Hindustani tradition tend to be passed down orally from teacher to student, Carnatic compositions are sometimes written down in a basic form of notation.

Identifying Features

One important characteristic of Indian music is that it utilizes a drone, or one or more notes that are constantly played in the background, usually by a string instrument known as a tamboura. The drone itself is somewhat hypnotic. Its purpose is to "frame" the music and to establish a base of notes around which the melody is played.

Another important aspect of Indian music is that it allows for creative improvisation by the musicians, within the rules of scale, melody, and rhythm. Because of this, two performances of the same composition by the same artist are never alike. Live concerts can often be very exciting because the musicians, including the drummers, engage in on-the-spot improvisation. Occasionally

A musician plays the tamboura.

when the improvisation reaches a climax, the audience breaks into applause and shouts words of encouragement. Most Indian classical ragas begin with a slow solo section called an *alap*. The *alap* is a type of introduction without percussion that sets the tone for the piece. It also allows the musician to improvise around the fixed notes, and introduces the basic scale and melodic content of the composition. After the *alap* is over, the percussion enters and the piece proceeds through several faster sections until it reaches an excited finale. As with music from other parts of the world, especially in the East, all musicians usually sing or play the same melody together in unison, without harmony or counterpoint.

Instruments

There is an incredibly wide range of musical instruments on the South Asian subcontinent. The most common ones in the Hindustani tradi-

Name _____ Date _____ Class _____

Lesson 8

Jayanthi is hailed as a great *vina* player. The *vina* is a revered instrument often associated with the Hindu goddess of knowledge, Saraswati.

tion are plucked stringed instruments such as the *sarod* and the sitar. The sitar was made popular in the West by Ravi Shankar, who once taught Indian music to George Harrison of the famous rock group The Beatles. There are bowed instruments such as the *sarangi;* wind instruments such as the *bansuri* bamboo flute; and many types of percussion. Indian musicians commonly play drums on the floor while sitting in a cross-legged position.

In Carnatic music, the most common instruments are the plucked *vina*, a beautiful and ancient instrument; the violin, which was borrowed from Europe and adapted to Indian music; the bamboo flute and a reed instrument called the *nadaswaram;* the double-headed barrel drum called the *mrdangam;* a clay pot called *ghatam*, which is played with the hands and the fingers; and the *kanjira*, a small lizard skin tambourine. (Many of the instruments mentioned above can be heard in the audio tracks that accompany this program.)

Modern/Popular Music

The most popular and best-selling songs in South Asia are found in movies. India has the world's largest film industry, centered in Mumbai (Bombay). Most movies in India are musicals. Film music retains a strong Indian flavor, but borrows very much from Western music in its use of instrumentation and arrangement. As in other parts of the East, rock music is often a favorite of young people, but there are also other forms of Western popular music heard and performed in India. Although music constantly evolves and changes, the musical legacy of South Asia is rooted in ancient and proud traditions that have survived and been passed down from generation to generation over thousands of years.

Ravi Shankar's daughter, Anoushka, continues her father's legacy by playing the sitar.

World Music: A Cultural Legacy

Name _____ Date _____ Class _____

Lesson 8

South Asia
Student Worksheet

DIRECTIONS: Read about the music of South Asia on pages 66–69. Then using the essay and, if necessary, your geography text as references, answer the following questions in the spaces provided.

1. The following phrases describe terms from the essay. Write the term that matches each definition.

   a. The rhythmic system in Indian music _____

   b. The melodic system (scales) in Indian music _____

   c. The North Indian style of Indian music _____

   d. A stringed instrument that plays a drone _____

2. Which important string instrument was made famous in the West by Ravi Shankar?
   _____

3. Which instrument was borrowed from Europe, and is now played in the classical music of India?
   _____

4. What are the most famous Indian drums?
   _____
   _____

5. Name and briefly describe three distinguishing features of South Asian music.
   _____
   _____
   _____
   _____
   _____
   _____
   _____

70   World Music: A Cultural Legacy

Name _____ Date _____ Class _____

Lesson 8

Music of South Asia

DIRECTIONS: As you listen to the music of South Asia on Disc Two, Tracks 7–13 (Cassette 2, Side A), answer the questions that follow in the spaces provided.

TRACK 7 PAKISTAN

Song "La Ilaha Il-Allah"
C P 1996, Green Linnet Records, Inc.
By: The Sabri Brothers

This is an example of *qawwali* music, devotional singing of the Pakistani Muslims. The music utilizes traditional voices, a chorus, and drumming and percussion, but also features a modern instrument, the electric bass.

1. Describe the musical relationship between the lead singer and the chorus in the song.

   _____

   _____

2. Select and list some words to describe the feeling of this song.

   _____

TRACK 8 INDIAN VOCAL RHYTHMS

Song "Konnakkol" (Percussion Language)
C P 1997, Music of the World
By: Karnataka College of Percussion

This piece begins like a spoken conversation among three percussionists and continues into individual musical sections with all three singers. The words they are saying reflect the names of different percussion sounds, such as could be played on a drum.

1. What is it about this song that is so unusual to your ears?

   _____

   _____

2. Can you tell that these men are accomplished drummers? Explain.

   _____

World Music: A Cultural Legacy

Name _____ Date _____ Class _____

Lesson 8

TRACK 9 BENGALI FOLK MUSIC

Song "Shola Gobe"
© ℗ 1990, Music of the World
By: Purna Das Baul Bengali folk ensemble

This is an Indian folk song, which speaks in poetic language. The words say that the world is an illusion. "Heavy rocks float on water; the mongoose has fallen in love with the snake. All that you see is not real."

1. In your own words, describe the sound and the quality of the singer's voice.

_____

TRACK 10 INDIAN HAMMERED DULCIMER

Song "Dhun in Misra Anandi"
© ℗ 1999, Music of the World
By: Tarun Bhattacharya and Bikram Ghosh

This is a semi-classical composition based on a North Indian folk song. It is played on a 100-string hammered dulcimer (santur), with tabla accompaniment.

1. Listen to the sound of the low drum as it rises and lowers in pitch. This drum is the tabla from North India. How do you think the musician gets the drum to go up and down in pitch?

_____

TRACK 11 SOUTH INDIAN FLUTE

Song "Kriti: Sobhillu saptasvara"
© ℗ 1999, Music of the World
By: N. Ramani and Trichy Sankaran

This recording features three musicians playing one of the most popular songs in the Carnatic (South Indian) repertoire.

1. From what you've learned about Indian music, all instruments usually play the same melody, rather than use harmony or counterpoint. In addition to the drum, what are the two instruments in this song?

_____

2. Which instrument do you think is leading the melody? Which instrument is quickly following, or echoing the lead instrument?

_____

72   World Music: A Cultural Legacy

Name _____ Date _____ Class _____

Lesson 8

TRACK 12 — THE SITAR

Song: "Rag Mishra Pahadi"
© ℗ 1987, 1994, Music of the World
By: Jagdeep Singh Bedi

After a short *alap* (introduction) on sitar, the flute and tabla join in the playing of this soft song.

1. The first minute of this song is an *alap*, or solo introduction. What effect does this have on the listener?

   _____
   _____

2. What role do you think the *alap* plays in the context of the entire piece?

   _____

3. If the song began right away with the drums, would the effect be different? Explain your answer.

   _____
   _____

TRACK 13 — NORTH INDIAN TABLA

Song: "Khandam"
© ℗ 1999, Music of the World
By: Bikram Ghosh

This selection highlights the mathematical and intellectual abilities of the drummer. Various rhythmic patterns are explored, and the drummer first speaks the drum notes before he plays them.

1. Tabla drums are two separate small drums played while sitting on the floor. How do you think the drummer is hitting these drums in order to produce such rapid-fire sounds?

   _____
   _____

2. Try to distinguish and describe each of the different sounds coming from these drums. How many different sounds can you count?

   _____
   _____

World Music: A Cultural Legacy

Name _____ Date _____ Class _____

Lesson 8

Exploring Regional Music
Student Activity 8

DIRECTIONS: Read the information below, then answer the questions that follow on a separate sheet of paper and be prepared to discuss your answers in class.

THE SITAR

Of all traditional world music instruments, the sitar is probably the best known. This fascinating instrument dates back to thirteenth-century India, yet it was modeled on much earlier folk instruments that originated in Persia. In Iran today, there is still a small string instrument with a long neck known as a *setar*.

The Indian sitar has a long neck fashioned from wood and a resonating chamber made of one half of a large dried gourd. There are six or seven main playing strings, which are plucked or strummed with a plectrum. The pitch of each string varies according to the particular raga being played. Four strings are usually used to play the melody while the others are strummed to create a constant drone. In addition, there are between 11 and 19 additional "sympathetic" strings. These strings are fastened to a separate bridge that runs underneath and diagonal to the main playing area. The tuned sympathetic strings vibrate even without being played. In this way they create an effect similar to an echo, or reverb.

Twenty movable brass frets are fastened to the sitar's long, hollow neck. These allow for tuning and modifying the pitch of the four playing strings. The frets are curved at the extremities, and this allows the musician to "pull" the strings across the frets in order to stretch the pitch of the note being played. This type of pitch bending is very characteristic of Indian music, and of Eastern music in general.

The world's most famous performer of the sitar is Ravi Shankar, a revered teacher, or guru, of Indian music traditions. George Harrison of The Beatles, however, played an important role in helping to introduce this instrument to the West. Harrison first heard a sitar being played at an Indian restaurant in England, and was immediately impressed. He soon began taking lessons from Ravi Shankar, and incorporated the sitar into several of The Beatles' popular songs. Since then, the sitar has become widely known outside of India, and is studied by thousands of musicians across the United States and Canada.

An example of sitar music can be heard on Glencoe's "World Music: A Cultural Legacy" audio program—Disc 2, Track 12 (Cassette 2, Side A).

QUESTIONS TO CONSIDER

1. A fret is a ridge that is fixed across the fingerboard of a stringed instrument. If a fret on a sitar is movable, and you move it farther away from where you are plucking the string, will the pitch get higher or lower? Why?
2. Considering what you've read about Indian music in this program, why do you think movable frets are so important on Indian string instruments? Explain.

Lesson 9

Music of East Asia

DIRECTIONS: Read the information below, and use it to complete the Lesson 9 Student Worksheet.

In the varied regions of East Asia, music shares similar structures and patterns, although regional differences are also common. Much of the traditional music in Japan and North Korea and South Korea was influenced by China, whose music dominated the area for many centuries. In East Asia today, however, all types of music are performed and enjoyed, including traditional folk music, Western classical music, opera, and more popular forms such as rock, pop, and New Age.

Chinese Classical Music

China's classical music is one of the most ancient music forms in the world. Its principles of composition and theory have remained relatively unchanged for thousands of years. According to an ancient legend, the emperor Huang Ti sent a special envoy deep into the mountains of western China and asked him to bring back certain fundamental pitches (notes) by which music could be made. After much searching, one day a mythological male phoenix (bird) appeared and sang a melody of six distinct tones. The male bird was answered by a female phoenix who sang six different notes. The messenger quickly cut different lengths of bamboo and matched them to the 12 tones he had heard the birds sing. In Chinese art music, these fundamental tones became known as the 12 *lü*, which correspond roughly to the 12-note chromatic scale that we use in Western music. Half of these notes were created yin (female) and half of them yang (male), so that a perfect balance of spiritual energy could be maintained. Later, individual scales were selected from the principal notes of the *lü* in order to form other melodic scales. The most important of these scales is the

Yin and yang are two opposing forces believed to be present in all of nature.

Bejing, or Peking, opera is widely regarded as the highest expression of Chinese culture. This is an opera performer.

World Music: A Cultural Legacy 75

Lesson 9

5-tone pentatonic scale, which is identical to the relationship of the five black notes of a piano. Today this same pentatonic scale is found throughout East Asia, and in many other places around the world.

Other Forms of Chinese Music

Chinese music may be considered in four general categories: ritual music, chamber music, Chinese opera, and folk and popular music. China's ritual music originated thousands of years ago with ancient government ceremonies and temple worship. Chamber music's oldest tunes date back to the Han dynasty (207 B.C.-A.D. 220). In addition to sung poems, there is another form of Chinese chamber music that can be referred to as "program" music. These texts often represent scenes from nature, and inspire images and portray sounds such as the galloping of horses, raindrops falling on leaves, birds swooping in the air, and so on. Although China's chamber music is soft and serene, Chinese operas are often noisy and wild. Stories are drawn from incidents in its vast history, or from legends involving demons, mythological creatures, ghosts, and evil magicians.

Although the folk music of China evolved over a long period of time, as with most forms of artistic expression, it was suppressed during the Cultural Revolution of 1966 to 1978. The effect of the Cultural Revolution on the arts was disastrous. The Chinese Communist government discouraged Western music and Chinese traditional music, closed down music schools and record companies, and allowed relatively little new music to be composed and performed. Fortunately, sanctions were eventually lifted, and today traditional and Western music are acceptable and encouraged. Pop music today has taken on many influences from the West, and China's performers of Western classical music rank among the best in the world.

Japanese musician Tadashi Tajir studied many years to become premier *shakuhachi* player.

Japanese Kabuki theater is a musical theater, filled with dance, instrumental music, and percussion.

East Asian Music Versus Western Music

There are several ways in which Asian music is different from music in Europe and the Americas. One major difference is that Western music uses chords. Chords consist of several notes played at the same time that have a harmonious relationship to one another. In our musical minds, these chords provide a tonal relationship within which a given melody is based. If you sing the melody of your favorite song, in the back of your mind you will "hear" the chords go by as you sing the song. As the notes of the melody move along, they have a direct relationship to the musical "colors" that are

Lesson 9

portrayed by chords that frame the melody line. This is what we are accustomed to in the West, and this is how we hear, perceive, and enjoy music.

In much of Asian music, though, there are no chords used. Instead, the concept of a melody that is interlocked directly with a chord structure does not exist. Each melodic instrument plays its own version of the same tune, and often adds subtle changes in the tone, color, and ornamentations of individual notes. Another important difference is that East Asian music often seeks the maximum effect possible from the least material. In Asia, ornamentation of notes adds greatly to the overall quality of the melodies. In arriving at a particular note, there may be ornamentation such as pitch bending, quavering, and upward or downward sliding. In general, much more emphasis is placed on the way a particular note is played rather than on how many notes are used. In other words, quality, not quantity, is most important.

In Japanese music, for example, every space of time in music is not necessarily filled because it is believed that the moments of silence between notes can be as powerful as the notes themselves. You may notice that this same approach is found in East Asian poetry, painting, and other

A musician plays the *erhu*.

forms of art. Instead of filling a poem with many words, a painting with big images, or a performance with non-stop sound, space is left open in order to appreciate the subtle pleasures of each element of the piece. In this way, traditional East Asian music may be considered an art form, and its purpose and execution differ greatly from music in the West.

East Asian Rhythm and Instruments

Rhythm in East Asian music is also highly developed. To a certain extent it is more developed than in the West, where beats are so steady that even a drum machine can be used to drive the melodies of many popular songs. In the East, drums and percussion instruments such as gongs, bells, clappers, and scrapers are commonly used. In the Koreas, the most popular drum is called a *chango*. It often plays exciting rhythms in triple meter. In Japan there is the *taiko* drumming tradition, in which large groups of musicians perform on cylindrical or barrel-shaped drums whose heads can be

Nihon Daiko is a troupe of musicians and dancers who play Japanese *taiko* drums.

World Music: A Cultural Legacy

Lesson 9

up to five feet in diameter. Not only must the musicians have an acute sense of rhythm, but they must also be in top physical shape since they often remain in strenuous physical positions during performances.

Chinese musical instruments are varied both in sound and in material of construction. Some well-known string instruments are a long zither known as a *ch'in,* a lute called a *p'ipa,* and a type of folk fiddle known as an *erhu.* Among wind instruments, bamboo flutes and panpipes are common, as well as the *sheng,* a type of mouth organ that uses reeds to produce its sound. In North and South Korea, one of the most popular string instruments is the *kayageum,* a zither made of 12 strings of twisted silk supported by movable, cone-like bridges.

East Asian Musical Traditions

In Tibet, once a free republic until it was annexed by China, an ancient type of religious chanting is carried out by Buddhist monks. It sounds very otherworldly because of the low pitches often sung. Through this style of "overtone" singing, the natural harmonic properties of the human voice are emphasized, so that a group of men singing only one note sounds like they are producing a chord of several notes.

Japan has a strong tradition based on the *shakuhachi,* an end-blown vertical bamboo flute. To an orchestral flutist in the West, a *shakuhachi* is very difficult to play since it has no mouthpiece to direct the air. Instead, the sound must be coaxed out of the bamboo reed by precise and very controlled blowing into the cavity of the flute. In addition to individual bodies of solo music, both the *shakuhachi* and the *shamisen* (a stringed lute) have been used to create traditional theater music. Although Japan is the most westernized East Asian nation, its people have managed to carefully cultivate their heritage, especially in the areas of music, theater, and other forms of cultural expression.

A musician plays the *kayageum.*

78   World Music: A Cultural Legacy

Name _____ Date _____ Class _____

Lesson 9
East Asia
Student Worksheet

DIRECTIONS: Read about the music of East Asia on pages 75–78. Then using the essay and, if necessary, your geography text as references, answer the following questions in the spaces provided.

1. In the Chinese 12-note system, six notes are male notes and six are female notes.
   a. What is the 12-note system called?
   b. What are the Chinese words for female and male energy?

   a. _____

   b. female energy = _____ male energy = _____

2. Name and explain two ways in which East Asian music is different from music in the West. Explain those differences.

Name _____ Date _____ Class _____

Lesson 9

Music of East Asia

DIRECTIONS: As you listen to the music of East Asia on Disc Two, Tracks 14-18 (Cassette 2, Side A), answer the questions that follow in the spaces provided.

TRACK 14 | JAPANESE FLUTE

Song "Sagari Ha" (Falling Leaf)
© ℗ 1991, 1994, Music of the World
By: Tadashi Tajima

In falling, a leaf is momentarily floating free from all restraints, headed for rebirth as newly decomposed nutrients for the tree. This composition shows how the cycle of life, death, and rebirth is an important concept of nature and Buddhism.

1. List a few elements of Western music that are not present in this piece.

   _____
   _____
   _____
   _____

TRACK 15 | JAPANESE DRUMMING

Song "Hachidan Uchi Daiko"
© ℗ 1990, Lyrichord Discs, Inc.
By: Soh Daiko

This *taiko* arrangement is based on the dynamic movements and double drumming style, which originated in Tokyo. There are several drummers and percussionists in this piece, and each beat is clearly heard.

1. Do you think the drumming patterns are well rehearsed, or are they improvised? Explain your answer.

   _____
   _____
   _____
   _____

80   World Music: A Cultural Legacy

Name _____ Date _____ Class _____

Lesson 9

TRACK 16 — CHINA

Song: "The Moon Over Wall Gate on the Frontier"
© ℗ 1994, Wind Records
By: Chinese Instrumental Ensemble

This melody is meant to recreate a soldier's feelings of homesickness as he gazes at the moon on a starry night.

1. Are the string instruments playing different melodies, or are they playing variations of the same melody? Explain.

   _____

   _____

2. Describe two percussion instruments heard in this song.

   _____

   _____

TRACK 17 — KOREA

Song: "Kayageum excerpt"
© ℗ 2000, Music of the World
By: San Won Park

This composition dates back many hundreds of years to the court period. The *kayageum*, a silk string zither, has movable bridges and is plucked and strummed with a plectrum.

1. The strings of the *kayageum* are made of silk. Describe the difference in sound texture between these strings and, say, the steel strings of a guitar.

   _____

   _____

   _____

   _____

   _____

World Music: A Cultural Legacy

Name _____ Date _____ Class _____

Lesson 9

TRACK 18 — TIBET

Song: "Kul Kyon Pan"
© ℗ 1998, Amiata Media Srl.
By: Monks of the Sera Jé Monastery

This composition is a Tibetan ritual song, sung in traditional overtone singing style. It has been used for special occasions such as births and deaths.

1. Put the main note aside and try to concentrate on the unusual sounds and different notes in this piece. Describe what you hear.

_____
_____
_____
_____
_____
_____
_____
_____
_____
_____
_____
_____

Name _____ Date _____ Class _____

Lesson 9

Exploring Regional Music
Student Activity 9

DIRECTIONS: Read the information below, then answer the questions that follow on a separate sheet of paper and be prepared to discuss your answers in class.

TAIKO AND *SHAKUHACHI*—DIVERGENT MUSIC STYLES FROM JAPAN

The Japanese people are known for having the most modernized and progressive Asian society, yet they are also passionate keepers of age-old traditions. Two styles of music, the Japanese drumming known as *taiko* and the notched flute known as *shakuhachi,* are both steeped in centuries of tradition, yet in musical form and in function, they are very different from each other.

Stories of the origin of *taiko* drums have been traced back to written documents of seventh-century Japan. Over the years the *taiko* became associated with mystical powers, which included the ability to communicate with and entertain the gods, the power to drive away swarms of insects, to bring about rain, and to inspire armies going off to battle. The drums themselves are barrel-shaped, covered with skin on both sides, and struck with wooden mallets. The deep bass tones and resonating percussive sounds that are produced from an ensemble of *taiko* drums are unique. The drum patterns are steady and pulsating, and they are often increased and decreased in volume to heighten the musical tension. The musicians often scream out verbal cues and words of encouragement as they play. The whole experience is very exciting and lively.

In contrast, solo music of the *shakuhachi* flute is quiet and meditative. It has no rhythm at all. There are gaps of silence in between musical passages, and the pace is relaxed and focused, not driving and pulsating. The *shakuhachi* music repertoire was made popular many centuries ago by Zen Buddhist monks who used flute playing as a tool for spiritual meditation and concentration. Several different styles of playing have evolved over hundreds of years, and the written notation of the music is retained on beautiful handmade scrolls. *Shakuhachi* music, when expertly played, can bring both the listener and the performer to a state of deep meditation and relaxation.

An example of taiko *drumming can be heard on Glencoe's "World Music: A Cultural Legacy" audio program—Disc 2, Track 15 (Cassette 2, Side A).*

An example of the solo shakuhachi *flute can be heard on Glencoe's "World Music: A Cultural Legacy" audio program—Disc 2, Track 14 (Cassette 2, Side A).*

QUESTIONS TO CONSIDER

1. Both the *shakuhachi* flute and *taiko* drum have connections to spirituality. Describe the connections for each instrument.

2. What is at least one major difference in the music of the two instruments?

Name _____ Date _____ Class _____

Lesson 10

Music of Southeast Asia

DIRECTIONS: Read the information below, and use it to complete the Lesson 10 Student Worksheet.

The nations of Southeast Asia form an ethnically rich region containing a diversity of languages, customs, musical instruments, and dances. Highly structured ensemble music developed in the royal courts of the region. The wealth of these courts supported the creation of expensive instruments, complex music, and stylized dances. This type of classical music from Southeast Asia is still widespread today, and is performed on local and international stages. Far from the elaborate court traditions, music in rural areas is often based on village life, and directly reflects monsoon seasons, agricultural cycles, and religious festivities. In temples, mosques, churches, and spirit shrines, traditional chants are still performed alongside age-old rituals.

Bronze, Bamboo, and Strings

One of the most identifying features of Southeast Asian music is the prevalence of metal gongs. The earliest gongs, made of bronze, date back to 2700 B.C. Today bronze gongs are still found throughout this region. Hill-dwelling people in Cambodia, Laos, and Vietnam play sets of bronze gongs, and similar instruments are used in lowland areas of Thailand, Myanmar, and Cambodia. Thousands of islands make up the rest of Southeast Asia, and in these regions, gongs play an important role in everyday music and are used for ceremonies and social celebrations. The most famous of these gongs are the gamelan ensembles of Indonesia and the *kulintang* traditions in Malaysia and the Philippines.

Bamboo is also an important material in the construction of musical instruments in Southeast Asia. Sections of bamboo are cut and carved into xylophone keys, flutes, resonating bodies for string instruments, and tubes and containers for shakers and percussion instruments. Bamboo is also used to construct panpipes and "mouth organs," sets of bamboo pipes that are lashed together and attached to a common air chamber. Wood is used for the faces and necks of string instruments and for the

Cambodian classical dance, represented by dancers performing graceful gestures in elaborate costumes, is a very important part of Cambodian culture.

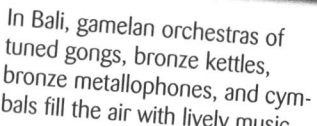

In Bali, gamelan orchestras of tuned gongs, bronze kettles, bronze metallophones, and cymbals fill the air with lively music.

84   World Music: A Cultural Legacy

Lesson 10

A musician plays the Vietnamese xylophone, made of bamboo.

bodies of drums, a wide variety of which are found in the area.

String instruments are very popular in Southeast Asia, and include lutes, zithers, fiddles, monochords, and other instruments. Nowadays most strings are made of steel or nylon, but there are instruments that still use silk strings, the most common material of the early days. In order to produce semitones and to tune to different modes, some string instruments have movable bridges. These often take the shape of inverted cones that lie flat against the soundboard and raise the string an inch or more from the base. By moving the individual bridges supporting each string, notes can be tuned precisely to any pitch. In some cases, slight variations of pitch of the same note are required in a song, and musicians must quickly move the bridge back and forth while they are playing in order to perform the piece properly.

A Wide Variety of Music Traditions

There is a strong tradition of string music throughout Vietnam. One of the most popular instruments is the *dan tranh,* a zither with 16 steel strings. The strings are stretched over a wooden soundboard and are divided by a series of movable wooden bridges. This instrument has a mesmerizing sound and expresses a wide range of feeling from melancholy to exciting and engaging.

Much less common than popular folk music, the *chau van* tradition of possession songs still exists in northern Vietnam. The earliest written reference of these songs dates back to 200 B.C. The song texts closely follow the movements of a person who has fallen into a trance. If someone drinks while in a trance, the song lyrics might immediately shift to a wine offering song. If he makes rowing movements with his arms, the singer will change the lyrics to a boater's song. These sudden changes require great skill and remarkable memory on the part of the singer.

In Laos, the most important instrument is the *khene,* a three-foot-long bundle of bamboo tubes enclosed in a carved wooden windchest. The musician blows air into the mouthpiece and manipulates fingerholes on the bamboo pipes in order to change tones. Each pipe has small metal reeds similar to those found in harmonicas and accordions, and not surprisingly, the *khene* sounds very much like both these instruments. The music is usually rhythmic and happy, and is often used to accompany dancers who incorporate playful hand and hip movements into their steps.

Farther south on the Indonesian island of Sumatra, there are ceremonial songs used for the unearthing of ancestral bones and songs that summon spirits to communicate through spirit mediums. For recreation, music is performed at home, on the streets, and at special all-night performances.

Bali, a small island east of Java has retained the Hindu traditions that were lost when Islam spread throughout the rest of Indonesia. Here, music

A musician plays the *dan tranh.*

World Music: A Cultural Legacy

Lesson 10

and dance are often performed outdoors at village temples. The most famous epic story is the *Ramayana,* a tale of a young prince who must rescue his beautiful wife from a demon king who kidnapped her. This prince does this with the help of an army of monkeys, led by the white monkey-God, Hannuman. As in the rest of Indonesia, the most important instruments in Bali are called gamelan. A gamelan is a type of metal gong made in different shapes and sizes to produce a variety of tones. A complete gamelan orchestra may consist of up to 40 musicians playing gongs, flutes, bowed instruments, drums; and one or more singers and dancers. Gamelan music was developed in Indonesia, although the use of metal gongs has existed throughout Southeast Asia for many centuries.

The Philippine archipelago consists of more than 7,000 islands, approximately 900 of which are inhabited. About half of the 75 million people in the Philippines live on the island of Luzon. The Philippines is the only Christian country in Asia, due to its colonization by Spain from 1565 to 1898. Because of this long affiliation, Spanish music influences are still evident in Philippine dance and in folk and popular music. Instruments like the *bandurria,* guitar, and castanets come directly from the Spanish tradition. Traditional music of the Philippines, however, mixes various types of metal gongs with bamboo flutes, bamboo xylophones, and drums. These instruments are more consistent with the music traditions of the rest of Southeast Asia.

Here, a Laotian musician plays the *khene.*

Outside Influences

Europeans colonized all of Southeast Asia except Thailand, known for centuries as the kingdom of Siam. In Myanmar the European piano is re-tuned and used for traditional Burmese music. Words from many foreign languages have come to denote native instruments in the region. Aside from the Western influence heard today in the pop music of Southeast Asia, the Philippines is the country that has been most influenced by music from the West. For many centuries, however, the primary outside musical influence came from China, and today traditional Chinese instruments are still played in Vietnamese and Thai fashion.

Although modern Western music is heard throughout Southeast Asia, it seems to live more on the fringes of society than it does in other cultures around the world. Perhaps because of the long history of classical court music, the wide variety of unique instruments, and the ethnic diversity of its population, the music of Southeast Asia has remained true to its roots, and continues to reflect the ancient legacy of its people.

Musician Phong Nguyen plays a Vietnamese lute.

Name _____ Date _____ Class _____

Lesson 10

Southeast Asia
Student Worksheet

DIRECTIONS: Read about the music of Southeast Asia on pages 84–86. Then using the essay and, if necessary, your geography text as references, answer the following questions in the spaces provided.

1. The peoples of Southeast Asia primarily practice the Muslim and Buddhist religions, except for two areas that practice other religions. Name these two countries and list their main religions.

   _____

   _____

2. In order for string instruments to play semitones, the pitch of each string must be adjustable. In the West, we do this with tuning pegs. Describe a common way this is achieved in Southeast Asia, and list several other areas of the world that also use this method of tuning.

   _____

   _____

   _____

   _____

3. Name two places covered in the essay on Southeast Asia where spirit intercession or trance is performed.

   _____

   _____

4. List other places in the world where trance is an important element of religion. Why do you suppose trance is prevalent in some cultures and hardly known at all in other cultures?

   _____

   _____

   _____

   _____

   _____

World Music: A Cultural Legacy

Name _____ Date _____ Class _____

Lesson 10

Music of Southeast Asia

DIRECTIONS: As you listen to the music of Southeast Asia on Disc Two, Tracks 19-24 (Cassette 2, Side B), answer the questions that follow in the spaces provided.

TRACK 19 THE *KHENE* FROM LAOS

Song "Lam Ploen"
© 1989, World Music Institute;
℗ 1996, Music of the World
By: Khamvong Insixiengmai Ensemble

After a free rhythm introduction, the music in this recording takes on a lively beat. The *khene* is a three-foot-long bundle of bamboo tubes.

1. What instrument does this sound remind you of?

   _____

   _____

2. Is there a drone note in this song?

   _____

   _____

TRACK 20 VIETNAMESE FOLK MUSIC

Song "Do Doc Do Ngang" (Boat Song)
© 1989, World Music Institute;
℗ 1997, Music of the World
By: Phong Nguyen

This is a South Vietnamese folk song about two young lovers who discuss the possibility of marriage some day.

1. Select some words to describe the mood of this song.

   _____

   _____

   _____

   _____

88 World Music: A Cultural Legacy

Name _____ Date _____ Class _____

Lesson 10

TRACK 21 JAVANESE GAMELAN

Song "Ladrang Galagothang"
ⓒ ℗ 1989, 1994, Music of the World
By: Palace musicians and singers

This piece contains lengthy gong phrases and has a stately mood. A gamelan orchestra often contains up to 40 instruments.

1. Keep track of the rhythm of the song. As it approaches the ending, what happens?

   _____
   _____

2. What effect does the final deep gong have on the listener?

   _____
   _____

TRACK 22 DRUMMING FROM VIETNAM

Song "Drum Improvisation"
ⓒ 1989, World Music Institute;
℗ 1997, Music of the World
By: Phong Nguyen

Various rhythmic techniques are used in this drum improvisation on four drums played in a ritual music style.

1. Is there a steady rhythm, or does the beat alternate throughout the piece?

   _____
   _____
   _____

2. In addition to the sticks hitting the drum skins, where else do the sticks strike from time to time?

   _____
   _____
   _____

World Music: A Cultural Legacy

Name _____ Date _____ Class _____

Lesson 10

TRACK 23 CAMBODIA

Song "Toch Yum"
© ℗ 1997, Music of the World
By: Sam Ang Sam

The name of this song means "the gibbon weeps." The piece is performed in a 16-beat rhythmic cycle.

1. In addition to the oboe-like reed instrument, try to identify all the other instruments in this piece.

_____
_____
_____
_____
_____
_____

TRACK 24 LAOTIAN FOLK MUSIC

Song "Lam Ban Xok"
© 1989, World Music Institute;
℗ 1996, Music of the World
By: Khamvong Insixiengmai Ensemble

This song represents a southern Laos vocal style, a duet between a man and woman.

1. Without knowing anything about this tradition, what type of dance movements do you think might be associated with this rhythm?

_____
_____
_____
_____
_____
_____

90   World Music: A Cultural Legacy

Name _____ Date _____ Class _____

Lesson 10

Exploring Regional Music
Student Activity 10

DIRECTIONS: Read the information below, then answer the questions that follow on a separate sheet of paper and be prepared to discuss your answers in class.

GAMELAN, THE GONGS OF INDONESIA

The word *gamelan* is used to describe an entire set or orchestra of percussion instruments, most of which are metal gongs and xylophones. The individual instruments themselves are also called gamelan; they are made in different shapes and sizes to produce varied tones. A complete gamelan orchestra may consist of up to 40 musicians playing metal gongs, flutes, bowed instruments, drums, and one or more singers and dancers. Gamelan music was developed in Indonesia, although the use of metal gongs has existed throughout Southeast Asia for many centuries. Before the fifteenth century, gamelan music was performed widely in Java. During the fifteenth century it spread to Bali, when many Javanese rulers fled there after the Muslim conquest of their land. From early times, gamelan music was associated with the royal courts and palaces of the sultans (kings). It was also used for religious ceremonies, and for dance-dramas and shadow-puppet performances, many of which are still performed today.

Gamelans are generally made of bronze, but other metals such as iron and brass are sometimes used. It takes a highly skilled artisan to produce a beautiful instrument that is well tuned and produces a rich sound. In order for the tones of the gamelan to resonate clearly, the metal gongs are suspended on a wooden frame. These frames are often painted in bright colors, and many feature carved wooden dragons and other creatures. The gongs vary in size from small, high-pitched metal bars measuring a few inches across to enormous gongs up to four feet high that produce deep bass tones. Although large orchestras of up to 40 people are sometimes assembled, there is no conductor, and all musicians sit facing the same direction. The main drummer, seated at the very center of the group, is responsible for providing the musical cues that mark tempos and signal the various sections of the music. The Javanese believe that the first gamelan was created in the third century by the god-king Sang Hyang Guru, who ruled his land from a high mountaintop. Today, despite modern influences and the spread of Western music, gamelan is still performed and enjoyed throughout Java, Bali, and other parts of Indonesia.

An example of gamelan music can be heard on Glencoe's "World Music: A Cultural Legacy" audio program—Disc 2, Track 21 (Cassette 2, Side B).

QUESTIONS TO CONSIDER

1. Describe a few ways in which a gamelan orchestra differs from an orchestra of Western classical music.

2. Throughout Indonesia, each major village has one or more official sets of gamelan. Do you think a gamelan orchestra would be difficult to take on an international tour? Explain your answer.

Name _____ Date _____ Class _____

Lesson 11
Music of Australia and Oceania

DIRECTIONS: Read the information below, and use it to complete the Lesson 11 Student Worksheet.

This lesson deals with the thousands of islands and atolls that make up Polynesia (from the Greek words *poly* for many and *nisi* for island), Melanesia (from *melani* for dark), and Micronesia (from *mikro* for small). This area also includes the large islands of Papua New Guinea, New Zealand, and the very largest island of them all, the continent of Australia.

The indigenous music traditions of Australia and Oceania are similar in that they convey elements of social structure, spirituality, religion, and everyday life. Unlike in Western cultures where music serves mostly as entertainment, this part of the world has traditionally used music as a way to maintain interpersonal relationships, to spread values about society, and to celebrate at their deepest levels life, death, peace, war, and other social events. In some areas and with certain types of songs, it is extremely important to sing correctly because it is believed that an imperfect performance may bring about physical harm to the performers themselves.

The Pacific Islands

Many of the native cultures of the Pacific islands suffered and almost collapsed under pressures from the British, French, and Spanish explorers of the late eighteenth century and the European missionaries who came after them. Hundreds of years after the missionaries first arrived, Tahiti and other islands in this area still sing songs called *himenes* that echo back to the musical structure of European religious hymns. The strong influence of earlier Christian singing may be heard here and also in Australian Aboriginal women's choirs.

Since in Papua New Guinea there are more than a thousand tribal groups speaking more than 700 languages and dialects, the island's music is also diverse. In the highlands, the most important traditional music function is called a *singsing*. A *singsing* is a large gathering of people who come to a central location from distant villages to compete and perform their own

Te Vaka plays original and contemporary Pacific music. Its members are from New Zealand.

particular music. Up until the early twentieth century, many of these tribes were enemies, cannibalism was common, and people from different tribes never met each other except in war. In the

92   World Music: A Cultural Legacy

Lesson 11

lowland areas of New Guinea however, the music takes a different form. It is generally more calm and incorporates wind instruments and drums such as the *garamut,* a wooden slit log that is hollowed out and slit in sections so as to create resonant tones when struck. The most remarkable wind instruments are the sacred bamboo flutes of the Sepik River area, which can reach lengths of up to six feet. These giant flutes are played only by men. Women are not even allowed to look at them.

Geographically speaking, Hawaii belongs to the cultural area of Polynesia, although its status as a state of the United States radically accelerated changes to its music and culture. Traditional music from Hawaii consisted of chants, and to this day, the accompanying poetry and hula dances are complex and rich. Contemporary Hawaiian folk music incorporates the guitar (introduced by Mexican immigrant workers in the early 1800s) and the famous ukulele, which was based on a Portuguese string instrument called the *braguinha.*

This pounder is used to beat the *garamut* slit drums.

This boy from New Guinea holds a drum.

This woman is playing a ukulele.

Australia and New Zealand

The native people of Australia are called Aborigines. Traditional Aboriginal music is strongly rhythmic, with a focus on natural sounds such as hand clapping, foot stomping, body slapping, and the clapping together of special wooden sticks known as *bilma. Bilma* are hand-carved in a way so that they emit different tones depending on how they are struck against each other. Chanting is a very important part of Aboriginal life. Traditional songs recount myths of ancient wanderers who traveled over the continent praising everything they encountered along the way, including animals, birds, and even rocks, plants, and watering holes. Each Aboriginal clan takes one of these elements as its totem, something that serves as an emblem or a revered symbol. Aboriginal song is arranged in a series of verses

Name _____ Date _____ Class _____

Lesson 11

An Aborigine plays the didgeridoo.

(some songs are extremely long), and the lyrics relate to a particular event or place associated with mythical and spiritual ancestor-beings. Through singing, dancing, art, body painting, and special ceremonies, Aborigines interact with all the natural elements around them, and in this way serve as active participants in the continuation and re-animation of all life-forms.

By far the most important and famous traditional instrument from Australia is the didgeridoo, a wooden trumpet made from the branch of a eucalyptus tree that has been hollowed out by termites. These days the didgeridoo is also made of bamboo, or any other kind of hollow tubular wood, metal, or plastic. In its traditional setting in the northern Australian area known as Arnhem Land, this unique instrument is traditionally played only by men. By properly blowing and singing into a didgeridoo, the performer is able to produce a wide variety of sounds, rhythms, and textures. The sound is very hypnotic, and is sometimes used as an inducement to achieve altered states of consciousness.

The native inhabitants of New Zealand, the Maori people, arrived from the Cook Islands between the tenth and fourteenth centuries. Musically speaking, the Maoris are still related to the cultures of the Cook Islands, Samoa, and Tahiti. The most important form of music for the Maori is a chant called *haka*. *Hakas* are sung for ceremonial and social events. They generally have a call-and-response pattern, and often include foot stomping, body thrusting, and exaggerated facial expressions. Today the Maori represent about only one-tenth of the population of New Zealand.

The popular music of Australia and New Zealand is far removed from the traditional music of the original inhabitants. Common folk instruments are the banjo, fiddle, button-accordion, tin whistle, guitar, and harmonica. Australian folk music tells stories that deal with social activities, ranching, work, and daily life. In addition to folk music, Australians and New Zealanders listen to and perform a wide range of music from classical to jazz, New Age, and rock.

Music in this part of the world is unique and displays a wide range of musical textures. From the otherworldly sound of a didgeridoo, to the tropical sway of Pacific Island string and choral music, to the steady rhythms of Australian Aboriginal rock-fusion, the music of this region has a distinct character, one which belongs only to this remote and beautiful part of the world.

Aboriginal musicians display their instruments.

94   World Music: A Cultural Legacy

Name _____ Date _____ Class _____

Lesson 11

Australia and Oceania
Student Worksheet

DIRECTIONS: Read about the music of Australia and Oceania on pages 92–94. Then using the essay and, if necessary, your geography text as references, answer the following questions in the spaces provided.

1. What other types of music at social gatherings does the *singsing* from Papua New Guinea remind you of? Explain your answer.

2. How does an Australian Aborigine use music differently than a musician in the West?

3. Chanting is very important in the music of Oceania. In modern Western society, when and where is group singing still found?

4. Why do you think group singing may be more common in the Pacific islands than in modern urban environments?

World Music: A Cultural Legacy

Name _____ Date _____ Class _____

Lesson 11

Music of Australia and Oceania

DIRECTIONS: As you listen to the music of Australia and Oceania on Disc Two, Tracks 25-29 (Cassette 2, Side B), answer the questions that follow in the spaces provided.

TRACK 25 AUSTRALIAN FUSION

Song "Spirits of the Sky"
ⓒ ⓟ 1997, Mastertech Pty Ltd
By: Uluru: Rhythms of the Rock

This modern piece was inspired by the spirits of the night sky who glide through the darkness. The Aboriginal didgeridoo is featured, along with other instruments.

1. Even though this piece uses modern electric instruments, it still conveys a mysterious sound. Why do you think this is so?

   _____
   _____
   _____
   _____

TRACK 26 SAMOA

Song "E keli"
ⓒ ⓟ 1997, ARC Music Productions Int.
By: Te Vaka

This piece features traditional slit drumming. The verses speak about the women on shore greeting men returning from fishing.

1. Describe the interaction between the male and female singers. What is this type of singing called?

   _____
   _____
   _____
   _____

96   World Music: A Cultural Legacy

Name _____ Date _____ Class _____

Lesson 11

TRACK 27 — FOLK MUSIC FROM VANUATU

Song: "Vanuatu"
© ℗ 1995, ARC Music Productions Int.
By: Fenes String Band

This is an example of popular string band music from Melanesia. This song is from the island of Vanuatu, and its lyrics boast about a diving competition.

1. What types of images and associations does this music call to mind?

   _____

   _____

2. Without truly knowing this culture, why do these associations and images seem so strong in your mind?

   _____

   _____

TRACK 28 — THE DIDGERIDOO

Song: "Didgeridoo Introduction"
© ℗ 2000, Mastertech Pty Ltd
By: Harry Wilson

The didgeridoo is possibly the world's oldest musical instrument. This track features a solo didgeridoo with accompanying clapping sticks, vocals, and the natural sounds of birds in the background.

1. How would you describe the sounds that come out of a didgeridoo?

   _____

   _____

2. Do you think the sounds produced by a didgeridoo are good for communicating with spirits? Explain your answer.

   _____

   _____

   _____

World Music: A Cultural Legacy

Name _____ Date _____ Class _____

Lesson 11

TRACK 29 — AUSTRALIAN FOLK MUSIC

Song "Bound for South Australia"
Ⓒ Ⓟ 1996, 1999, Mastertech Pty Ltd
By: The Aussie Bush Band

This is a well-known Australian folk song set in a modern arrangement. The singer talks about nostalgia and yearning to return to South Australia.

1. What kind of images and associations does this song evoke?

   _____
   _____
   _____
   _____
   _____
   _____

2. Does this music remind you of any other type of music? Explain.

   _____
   _____
   _____
   _____
   _____
   _____
   _____
   _____

Name _____ Date _____ Class _____

Lesson 11

Exploring Regional Music
Student Activity 11

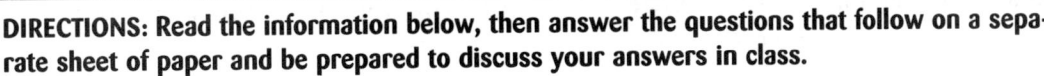

DIRECTIONS: Read the information below, then answer the questions that follow on a separate sheet of paper and be prepared to discuss your answers in class.

THE DIDGERIDOO AND CIRCULAR BREATHING

Of all the world's traditional ethnic instruments, the didgeridoo is surely one of the most unusual. Since the Aborigines in Australia are considered to be the oldest living people on the earth, the didgeridoo may be the earth's oldest musical instrument still in use. This humble instrument consists of nothing more than a eucalyptus tree branch, which has been hollowed out by very hungry termites! After collecting the hollowed logs, which vary in length according to the pitch they produce, Aborigines clean and prepare the logs for use by applying beeswax to the end of the tube that touches the mouth. (Didgeridoos are often carved with intricate designs of totems and depictions of animals, and they are painted in bright colors). These days, commercially made didgeridoos are also made of bamboo, plastic, and other types of wood.

Although the instrument itself is very simple, the playing techniques used and the sounds that are produced can be quite complicated. Since the instrument is basically a hollow tube without a mouthpiece, merely blowing air into it will produce little or no sound. Instead, you must use a combination of lip vibrations, throat sounds, and tongue movements to coax the sound out. It takes some practice before you can get a good tone. Previous experience on a brass instrument such as the trumpet speeds up the process of learning. By properly blowing and singing into a didgeridoo, the performer is able to produce a wide variety of sounds, rhythms, and textures.

Then comes the hard part—circular breathing. Circular breathing is blowing air out while you breathe in at the same time! As air is forced through the lips into the instrument, the player simultaneously takes air into the chest cavity through the nostrils and stores it up by puffing up the cheeks. The air supply continues to be replenished in this way without ever stopping the sound of the music. This process can go on almost indefinitely.

In Aboriginal culture, the use of the didgeridoo is essential in spiritual ceremonies, many of which feature several musicians performing on the didgeridoo, percussion, and voice for as many as eight hours without interruption. Music in Aboriginal Australia relates the journeys and actions of the ancestor spirits, who are believed by the Aborigines to have created all life on the earth and who laid down guidelines for social, political, and religious acitivities.

An example of didgeridoo music can be heard on Glencoe's "World Music: A Cultural Legacy" audio program—Disc 2, Track 28 (Cassette 2, Side B).

QUESTIONS TO CONSIDER

1. Do you think the concept of circular breathing is related in any way to the religious beliefs of the Aborigines? How? Why?
2. The didgeridoo produces only one note, which could be referred to as a drone. Do you think a drone is conducive to concentration and meditation? Can you think of other examples and uses of music in which a drone is used for prayer? Explain.

GLOSSARY OF MUSIC TERMS

Aborigines: native people of Australia

accordion: a portable keyboard wind instrument in which the wind is forced past free metallic reeds by means of a hand-operated bellows

alap: a slow solo introduction in Indian classical music that sets the tone for the piece

altiplano: the high plain of the Andes mountains of South America

bagpipe: one of the earliest instruments from Europe; the bag is usually made from an animal's stomach lining, and hollow sticks with finger holes are connected to it in order to produce sound

balafon: a West African wooden xylophone with gourd resonators

balalaika: a Russian string instrument that has a triangular wooden body and from two to four strings

ballad: a slow romantic or sentimental song

bandoura: a large short-necked lute from Russia

bandurria: Spanish stringed instrument

banjo: a string instrument with a long narrow fretted neck and a small body; it usually has five strings plucked or strummed with the fingers.

bansuri **flute:** a transverse bamboo flute from India

batá: a double-headed drum of African descent used when performing Santería music in Cuba

bellows: a device for expanding and contracting air for wind instruments

bhajans: modern devotional songs among the Hindu

bilma: Aboriginal wooden sticks used as percussion

blues: a type of American song expressing a mood of longing or melancholy

bodhran: a large Irish frame drum played with a small double-headed stick

bongos: a pair of small tuned drums played with the fingers and used especially in the Caribbean

bossa nova: a popular Brazilian song form with an interesting rhythm and jazz-like improvisations

bouzouki: a long-necked string instrument from Greece

braguinha: a small Portuguese string instrument

Cajuns: descendants of French Acadian exiles

call-and-response: a type of singing in which a leader sings a phrase and the entire group sings a response

calypso: a song form from the West Indies played on steel drums

Carnatic: of, or relating to, South India

100   World Music: A Cultural Legacy

Celtic music: traditional music from Ireland, Scotland, and the British Isles using instruments such as bagpipe, harp, and fiddle

chango: a popular drum from Korea

chanter: a pipe on a bagpipe that plays the melody

charango: a small, 10-stringed guitar-like instrument from the northern Andes region of South America; the body is made of wood or armadillo shell

chastushka: a type of Russian folk song that consists of short verses sung, composed, and improvised mostly by females

chau van: tradition of possession songs from northern Vietnam

ch'in: a long zither from China

cimbalom: a hammered dulcimer from eastern Europe

circular breathing: blowing air out while you breathe in at the same time

cobza: an eastern European lute

conga: a tall narrow-headed drum played with the hands

cordillera: a group of mountain ranges forming a mountain system of great length

counterpoint: two or more instruments playing different melodic lines at the same time

dan tranh: a zither with 16 steel strings from Vietnam

dastgah: melody based on a melodic mode from Iran

derdeba: a North African ceremony held to placate spirits

didgeridoo, didgeridu: a wooden trumpet made from the branch of a eucalyptus tree that has been hollowed out by termites

double bass: the largest instrument of the violin family; usually having four strings tuned in fourths and a range of about three octaves

drone: one or more notes that are constantly played in the background, usually by a string instrument

drones: the pipes on a bagpipe that produce one or more steady drone notes

dulcimer: an instrument with strings that are stretched over a fretted soundbox and played by plucking or strumming

dumbek (tombak): a metal or ceramic-bodied drum that can produce a loud, piercing sound

erhu: a type of Chinese folk fiddle

Farsi: the language of Persia and Iran

fiddle: a bowed stringed instrument often used to accompany dancing

finale: the last section of an instrumental musical composition

flamenco: a vigorous rhythmic music and dance style of the Andalusian Gypsies of Spain, which has distinct Arab influence

folk music: traditional music of a particular culture that is passed down by oral tradition

frets: a series of ridges of metal, ivory, or other material fixed across the fingerboard of a string instrument

fusion: a merging of several types of music into a unified form

gamelan: a set of tuned bronze metal instruments

gardon: a type of cello played by hitting the strings with a stick

garamut: a wooden slit log from Papua New Guinea that is hollowed out and slit in sections so as to create different tones when struck

gauchos: cowboys from the plains of Argentina

gospel music: a style of American sacred singing based on a message concerning Christ, the kingdom of God, and salvation

Gregorian chant: a type of liturgical chant with free rhythm

griots: oral historians and musicians from West African nations, who transmit information by performing at ceremonies and social events

haka: a Maori chant sung for ceremonial and social events

harmony: the organization of different pitches into chords

himenes: songs or hymns from Oceania that have European Christian roots

Hindustani: of, or relating to, North India

horsehead fiddle: a string instrument of Tuva and Mongolia

hosho: a small dried gourd, filled with seeds or pebbles, which is shaken as a percussion instrument in southern Africa

hula: a mime-like Polynesian dance accompanied by chants and rhythmic drumming

hurdy-gurdy: a drone instrument bowed by a rotating wheel

improvisation: the ability to create or play music spontaneously, without following written music

indigenous: something that originates or is produced naturally in a particular region

iyá: a large Afro-Cuban drum, which it is believed, communicates directly with spirits

jaw harp: an instrument usually made of metal, which uses the human mouth as a resonator

jazz: a type of American music that is characterized by improvisation

kachina: Native American spirit of the dead who, it is believed, assists people in their struggle for survival

kanjira: a small lizard skin tambourine from south India

kartal: small tuned cymbals from India

kayageum: a Korean zither made of 12 strings of twisted silk supported by movable bridges

khene: a Laotian reed instrument consisting of a three-foot long bundle of bamboo tubes enclosed in a carved wooden windchest

konnakkol: a language of spoken percussion notes from India

kora: a 21-stringed harp from West Africa

krar: a stringed instrument from Ethiopia that has a sound similar to a banjo

lament: an important musical form used especially at weddings and funerals, characterized by loud wailing

lojki: wooden spoons used as percussion instruments in Russia

lü: fundamental tones in Chinese art music that correspond roughly to the 12-note chromatic scale of Western music

lute: a popular stringed instrument in Renaissance Europe; descended from the Middle Eastern 'ud

maqam (makam): melody based on a melodic mode known in the Arab countries and Turkey

mariachi: Mexican music that utilizes string and brass instruments, along with tight vocal harmonies

marimba: a xylophone made of wooden keys and suspended tubes or gourds, which amplify the sound

mbira: an African instrument made from a small wooden box or gourd with strips of iron mounted on top; a thumb piano

merengue: a popular Dominican and Haitian ballroom dance with a limping step

mrdangam: a double-headed drum from southern India

nay (nai): an end-blown Middle Eastern flute with a very breathy tone

ndongo: an Ugandan string instrument

Norteño: an accordion-based style of music played mostly on the Texas/Mexican border

ocarinas: enclosed wind instruments with several holes, usually made of clay or wood

orishas: Afro-Cuban deities, which are also associated with Catholic saints

oud ('ud): a Middle Eastern pear-shaped lute

overtone singing: a type of singing whereby one singer can produce two tones simultaneously

pampas: the grass-covered plain of South America

panpipes: an ancient wind instrument that consists of a graduated series of short vertical flutes bound together

World Music: A Cultural Legacy **103**

pans: *See steel drums*

percussion: rhythmic instruments, like drums or shakers that are struck with a stick, the hands, or some other object

p'ipa: a well-known string instrument from China

plectrum: a small thin piece of ivory, wood, metal, horn, quill, or other material used to play string instruments

polka: a couple dance of Bohemian origin combining three steps and a hop

polyphonic: consisting of two or more distinct melodies combined into a unified musical composition

polyrhythm: the layering and interlocking of two or more rhythms at the same time

qaraqeb: large metal clappers or castanets from North Africa, which beat out a steady, pulsating rhythm

qawwali: a popular form of Pakistani Muslim devotional music

quena: a vertical end-notched flute played in the Andes

Quran: ancient book of the Muslim religion, which when read is chanted in a particular style

raga: one of the ancient traditional melodic patterns of Hindu music; something between a simple scale and a complete melody

rai: a rhythmic and very danceable music from North Africa, combining traditional and modern instruments and led by a talented and versatile singer

Ramayana: a Hindu tale of a young prince who must rescue his beautiful wife from a demon king who kidnapped her

rap: modern music that is characterized by spoken rhythmic words

repertoire: a list of musical works available for performance

rumba: a Cuban dance marked by strong movements

salsa: hypnotic dance music of Cuban and Puerto Rican origin based on African rhythms and using strings, drums, brass, and percussion

samba: a Brazilian dance and music form of African origin

Santería: Afro-Cuban spirit worship music

santur: a type of hammered zither played in Indian music

sarod: plucked stringed instrument common from North India

saz: a Turkish lute, which has a long slender neck and produces a bright, slightly buzzing sound

semitones: musical notes that correspond to the notes that lie between the black and white keys of a piano

setar: a long-necked lute from Iran

shakuhachi: a Japanese vertical bamboo flute with five fingerholes

shamisen: a stringed lute from Japan

shékeres: percussion instrument made of a dried gourd and surrounded by beads

sheng: a type of mouth organ that uses reeds to produce its sound

siku: See *zampoña*

singsing: a large gathering of tribespeople from Papua New Guinea who compete and perform music

sintir: a three stringed, skin-faced lute from Morocco

sitar: plucked stringed instrument from North India made popular in the West by Ravi Shankar

slit drums: hollowed giant logs that were used as a rhythmic communication system in Africa

soca: a popular music from the Caribbean played on steel drums

steel drums: percussion instruments made of oil barrels and tuned to a definite pitch

tabla: a pair of drums with tunable heads from North India

taiko: large Japanese drums; the style of music characterized by these drums

tala: an Indian rhythmic structure that consists of a fixed number of soft and hard beats

talking drum: double-headed drum from Africa that is played by squeezing the rope that joins the two heads

tamboura: an Indian musical instrument of the lute type, but without frets; used only to produce a drone

tango: a romantic and traditional music style from Argentina

Tex-Mex music: See *Norteño*

throat singing: See *overtone singing*

totem: an item that serves as an emblem or a revered symbol

uilleann pipes: a type of bagpipe

ukulele: a small Hawaiian guitar plucked or strummed with the fingers

valiha: a tubular bamboo zither from Madagascar

Vedas: ancient books from the Hindu religion, which when read are chanted in a particular style

vocables: vowel sounds with no real meaning

vodoun (voodoo): African-derived spirit worship from Haiti

waltz: a round dance in 3/4 time

washboard: a percussion instrument used in Cajun and early country music

yang: masculine and positive energy in nature, which according to traditional Chinese cosmology combines with the feminine yin to produce all matter

Yoruba: people, religion, and language primarily of Nigeria

yumbo: an ancient Ecuadorian rhythm played on a type of pentatonic panpipe

zampoña: bamboo panpipes from the Andes region of South America

zither: a stringed instrument with a shallow soundboard, played with the fingers, or a pick

zydeco: Cajun music's more modern cousin, which sometimes borrows a bit from blues and rock and roll

Appendix of Countries

The United States and Canada

Latin America
Antigua and Barbuda, Argentina, Bahamas, Barbados, Belize, Bolivia, Brazil, Chile, Colombia, Costa Rica, Cuba, Dominica, Dominican Republic, Ecuador, El Salvador, Grenada, Guatemala, Guyana, Haiti, Honduras, Jamaica, Mexico, Nicaragua, Panama, Paraguay, Peru, Puerto Rico, Saint Kitts and Nevis, St. Lucia, Saint Vincent and the Grenadines, Suriname, Trinidad and Tobago, Uruguay, Venezuela, Virgin Islands

Europe
Albania, Andorra, Austria, Belarus, Belgium, Bosnia and Herzegovina, Bulgaria, Croatia, Cyprus, Czech Republic, Denmark, Estonia, Finland, France, Germany, Greece, Hungary, Iceland, Ireland, Italy, Latvia, Liechtenstein, Lithuania, Luxembourg, Macedonia, Malta, Moldova, Monaco, Netherlands, Norway, Poland, Portugal, Romania, San Marino, Slovakia, Slovenia, Spain, Sweden, Switzerland, Ukraine, United Kingdom, Vatican City, Yugoslavia

Russia

North Africa, Southwest Asia, and Central Asia
Afghanistan, Algeria, Armenia, Azerbaijan, Bahrain, Egypt, Georgia, Iran, Iraq, Israel, Jordan, Kazakhstan, Kuwait, Kyrgyzstan, Lebanon, Libya, Morocco, Oman, Qatar, Saudi Arabia, Syria, Tajikistan, Tunisia, Turkey, Turkmenistan, United Arab Emirates, Uzbekistan, Yemen

Africa South of the Sahara
Angola, Benin, Botswana, Burkina Faso, Burundi, Cameroon, Cape Verde, Central African Republic, Chad, Comoros, Congo, Democratic Republic of the Congo, Côte d'Ivoire, Djibouti, Equatorial Guinea, Eritrea, Ethiopia, Gabon, Gambia, Ghana, Guinea, Guinea-Bissau, Kenya, Lesotho, Liberia, Madagascar, Malawi, Mali, Mauritania, Mauritius, Mozambique, Namibia, Niger, Nigeria, Rwanda, Sao Tome and Principe, Senegal, Seychelles, Sierra Leone, Somalia, South Africa, Sudan, Swaziland, Tanzania, Togo, Uganda, Zambia, Zimbabwe

South Asia
Bangladesh, Bhutan, India, Maldives, Nepal, Pakistan, Sri Lanka

East Asia
China, Japan, Mongolia, North Korea, South Korea, Taiwan

Southeast Asia
Brunei, Cambodia, Indonesia, Laos, Malaysia, Myanmar, Philippines, Singapore, Thailand, Vietnam

Australia and Oceania
Australia, Federated States of Micronesia, Fiji Islands, Kiribati, Marshall Islands, Nauru, New Zealand, Palau, Papua New Guinea, Samoa, Solomon Islands, Tonga, Tuvalu, Vanuatu

Answer Key

LESSON 2 MUSIC OF THE UNITED STATES AND CANADA

Student Worksheet

1. French
2. Norteño or Tex-Mex music (sung in Spanish); Native American music (sung in vocables)
3. Possible answers: racial discrimination, poverty, forced labor, and so on
4. blues has a strong steady beat; most people can relate to hard times and difficulties in life; use of familiar instruments such as guitar and harmonica
5. Possible answers: Native American music was not written down, it was passed on through oral tradition; In many cases Native Americans were forcibly prevented from performing their own music; European instruments began to take hold in the Americas; Christian music was taught and fostered among Native Americans.
6. through the spread of intertribal music; through the many powwows that are held throughout the country, and which are open to the general public
7. Early jazz forms are Ragtime, Swing, Bebop, Big Band, and Dixieland. A modern jazz form is "Smooth" Jazz.

Audio Activity

TRACK 1 CAJUN MUSIC

1. the fiddle (violin); The accordion also plays an important role.
2. a two-step

TRACK 2 THE BANJO

1. The musician is strumming with up and down motions. The speed could never be achieved if the strings were strummed in only one direction.

TRACK 3 NATIVE AMERICAN POWWOW MUSIC

1. jingle bells and gourd shakers (maracas)

TRACK 4 NATIVE AMERICAN FLUTE

1. Answers will vary, but may include words such as sad, painful, lonely, gentle, soft, spiritual, and so on.

TRACK 5 THE BLUES

1. The electric guitar plays the responses. It serves as a filler between the singers' verses, it engages the ear and moves the music forward, and it encourages the next line by the singer.

TRACK 6 CANADIAN FOLK MUSIC

1. the sung refrain "Oh, I may never leave again"
2. They give the listener a point of reference; something to hum; something that makes the song "catchy."

Exploring Regional Music
Student Activity 2-A

1. The Cajuns (slang for Acadians) were French settlers who arrived on the shores of Nova Scotia. They were eventually evicted by British colonizers and forced to leave the area. After years of wandering, they found their way to the French colony of Louisiana.
2. Possible answers: Cajuns share a strong cultural identity and a common French language, and they live in a small geographic area.
3. Possible answers: the French language, dances such as waltzes and two-steps, the use of the washboard as a percussion instrument, their popularity in modern media

Reminder: *An example of Cajun Music can be heard on Glencoe's "World Music: A Cultural Legacy" audio program–Disc One, Track 1 (Cassette 1, Side A).*

Exploring Regional Music
Student Activity 2-B

1. Possible answers: It is performed almost entirely through singing; harmony is generally not used; men traditionally do the singing; non-translatable syllables called vocables are used in singing; similar types of dances and ceremonies are shared.

2. Possible answers: Music is passed on through oral tradition from generation to generation; there is a strong cultural identity attached to their music; Native Americans often live on reservations and live a culturally homogeneous lifestyle; young people grow up hearing traditional music and dance.

Reminder: *An example of Native American powwow music can be heard on Glencoe's "World Music: A Cultural Legacy" audio program—Disc One, Track 3. The Native American flute is featured on Disc One, Track 4 (Cassette 1, Side A).*

LESSON 3 MUSIC OF LATIN AMERICA

Student Worksheet

1. native indigenous peoples, European settlers, Africans who were forced into slavery and brought to Latin America
2. Native Americans: flutes, panpipes, trumpets, percussion; Europeans: string instruments, the concept of harmony, brass instruments; Africans: marimba (xylophone), drums, percussion, steel drums
3. the *charango,* a small mandolin made from the shell of an armadillo
4. in the Andean countries; Ecuador, Peru, Colombia, Chile, Argentina, Bolivia
5. Gauchos are the South American equivalent of cowboys, and they tend cattle on the vast plains (pampas) of Argentina.
6. the guitar

Audio Activity

TRACK 7   CUBA

1. percussion instruments such as congas, bongos, timbales, and shakers and scrapers; piano; acoustic bass; and a brass section including several trumpets, trombones, and saxophones
2. The brass section plays in opposition to the main beat, on the weak beat. In musical terms, this is called syncopation.

TRACK 8   PUERTO RICAN FOLK MUSIC

1. The drums and percussion are African in origin. The string instrument is of Spanish origin.
2. The lead singer sings a melody or an entire verse (call) and the chorus sings one or two lines in response to it.

TRACK 9   BRAZIL

1. Possible answers: soft, sad, romantic, gentle, tropical. Encourage students to explain the feelings that are evoked through this rhythm.

TRACK 10   ECUADOR

1. It is pre-Columbian, dating back to before the arrival of the Spaniards to the Americas. (Note the lack of string instruments.) Therefore, it is influenced by Native American music.
2. Possible answers: Native American powwow music, a heartbeat

TRACK 11   MEXICO

1. Absolutely; the lead singer is answered by the chorus.
2. In almost all cases, instrumental solos (and even sung verses) are improvised. Student explanations will vary.

TRACK 12   PERU

1. The harp and other string instruments were European inventions.
2. There are two flutes. Student explanations will vary.

Exploring Regional Music
Student Activity 3-A

1. Colombia, Ecuador, Peru, Bolivia, Chile, Argentina, and a small part of Venezuela
2. Ancient Andean music was used only for religious and ceremonial purposes; only percussion and wind instruments were used; flutes and panpipes were made from bamboo. Today we largely use music for recreation and social enjoyment. We use many different types of musical instruments, made from woods, metals, and many other materials.

Reminder: *An example of Andean panpipe music can be heard on Glencoe's "World Music: A Cultural Legacy" audio program—Disc One, Track 10 (Cassette 1, Side A).*

Exploring Regional Music
Student Activity 3-B

1. The three drums interact with one another through a system of cues given by the largest drum, the *iyá*.
2. Yoruba is the language of Nigeria. It is used in Afro-Caribbean spiritual traditions such as Santería.

LESSON 4 MUSIC OF EUROPE

Student Worksheet

1. flamenco music from Spain
2. Possible answers: bagpipe, harp, fiddle
3. The geography of Europe has tended to isolate and separate cultures, allowing for traditional cultural values to remain strong. Europeans embrace and foster local customs, languages, and music as a statement of their identities. There have been many outside influences (Celts from the north, Arabs from the south) that have had strong regional impacts.
4. wind instruments such as natural horns, flutes, bagpipes
5. the guitar, drums, bowed string instruments, the piano, reed instruments

Audio Activity

TRACK 13   SPANISH FUSION

1. Answers will vary, but may include the following: It brings about tension and makes the listener eager to hear more, it provides a forward momentum, and so on.

TRACK 14   SWEDEN

1. There are regular periods of silence, which is unusual in most music from the West.
2. Answers will vary. Possible answers: scary, spooky, mysterious, tense, alert, and so on

TRACK 15   ROMANIA

1. Students will most likely think of country people or gypsies. Answers should focus on the simple, yet unique sounds of the song.
2. Possible answers: funny, light, silly, entertaining, happy, dance-like, and so on

TRACK 16   THE BRITISH ISLES

1. the guitar

TRACK 17   BRITTANY

1. Answers may vary, but should focus on the following: The song repeats the same short melody over and over; there is only one melody in the whole song; the rhythm is quick and the singing is very fast.

TRACK 18   BULGARIA

1. bells, drum, percussion shakers

TRACK 19   SICILY

1. bass, tambourine, drums, violin, saxophone

Exploring Regional Music
Student Activity 4-A

1. Learning through oral tradition and from one's family members is an old European custom, and aside from Native American traditions, it is not commonly employed in the United States and Canada. Encourage students to discuss the pros and cons of family learning versus school learning.
2. Answers will vary but may include religious activities, wedding parties, birthday celebrations, and so on.

Reminder: *An example of Romanian Gypsy music can be heard on Glencoe's "World Music: A Cultural Legacy" audio program–Disc One, Track 15 (Cassette 1, Side A).*

Exploring Regional Music
Student Activity 4-B

1. The distance from the southern coast of Ireland to the northern coast of Spain is approximately 600 miles over water. The Celtic culture spread from the British Isles across the English Channel to France, and then to Spain. Students may suggest that Celtic influences easily traveled along the coasts of France and Spain.
2. Possible answers: The accordion is probably the most widely used, and is found throughout Europe, the Americas, Australia, Africa, and Asia. The bagpipe is also widespread in Europe and is found on several continents.

Reminder: *An example of Celtic music from Ireland can be heard on Glencoe's "World Music: A Cultural Legacy" audio program—Disc One, Track 16 (Cassette 1, Side A). Track 17 is a Celtic song from Brittany.*

LESSON 5 MUSIC OF RUSSIA

Student Worksheet

1. See student essay for descriptions. Possible answers include:

a) traditional songs yielding magic powers to ward off evil spirits

b) songs used for planting and harvesting

c) songs to engage astronomical cycles

d) epic tales performed at weddings

e) laments used at weddings and funerals

f) *chastushka* social songs

g) Tuvan throat singing used by herders, and horse-related songs

2. This question is meant to draw on the students' imaginations and to contrast stereotypes with factual reality. Encourage your students to discuss their preconceptions, and how they may have been supported or diminished by the information in the essay.

3. Student answers will vary. Students should explain their choices.

Audio Activity

TRACK 20   RUSSIA

1. The changes in speed create tension, and usually make the listener want to hear more. The slow sections of this song evoke a bit of sadness or nostalgia.

TRACK 21   TUVA

1. Yes, all the musicians are playing and singing the same melody. This is called unison.

2. The strings play a drone when the singer begins the whistling sounds of his throat singing.

TRACK 22   RUSSIAN CHORAL MUSIC

1. For many people, the song transmits a solemn, strong mood. It sounds like religious music, or perhaps holiday music. Encourage students to express themselves by selecting words that convey the mood of the music.

TRACK 23   RUSSIAN POLKA

1. The other two instruments are the flute and bass.

Exploring Regional Music
Student Activity 5

1. As nomads, shepherds are constantly traveling, taking only what they need with them as basic necessities. It would be difficult to travel on foot or horseback with musical instruments.

2. Shepherds travel great distances with their flocks and are alone for long stretches of time. It is believed that this style of singing developed as a way to pass the time by singing a melody and an accompanying note at the same time.

3. Shepherds use throat singing to entertain themselves during their long solo journeys.

Reminder: *An example of Tuvan throat singing can be heard on Glencoe's "World Music: A Cultural Legacy" audio program—Disc One, Track 21 (Cassette 1, Side B).*

LESSON 6 MUSIC OF NORTH AFRICA, SOUTHWEST ASIA, AND CENTRAL ASIA

Student Worksheet

1. Farsi

2. Possible answers: All musicians play the same basic melody; there is generally no harmony; there is a strong use of improvisation; each melody is based on a specific melodic mode *(maqam, makam, dastgah)*; musicians play semitones (the notes between the black and white keys on a piano); rhythm consists of many variations of combinations of strong and weak beats.

3. Morocco is Spain's closest African neighbor.

4. the guitar

Audio Activity

TRACK 24 MOROCCO

1. The other sounds are voices, metal clappers (castanets), and hand claps.

TRACK 25 ISRAEL

1. Answers may vary, but may include that it creates tension; that it lays a foundation for the improvisation; that it allows for the full effect of the improvisation to be felt by the listener, and so on. Allow students to express themselves freely, as there is no "correct" answer here.

TRACK 26 AFGHANISTAN

1. It has a bright, metallic tone since it is played with a plectrum. Playing with the fingertips would produce a softer, darker tone.

TRACK 27 IRAN

1. There are two string instruments called *setars*. They exchange melody lines from one to the other, and sometimes play together.

2. Answers will vary, but in describing the periods of silence, students may use words such as mysterious, serious, reflective, peaceful, and so on. Allow the students to express themselves freely.

TRACK 28 ARMENIA

1. Nine beats; If students try to tap out the rhythm of the song, sometimes their taps will "fit" and sometimes they will not; that is, the "odd" ninth beat will be "felt" when the hand is in an upstroke, rather than on the downstroke.

2. The lone clarinet plays an improvisation, a melody made up on the spot.

TRACK 29 TURKEY

1. As with most music of this region, the other instruments play in echoing fashion the same melody sung by the vocalist.

2. All the instruments play the same notes, although they sometimes ornament or embellish them slightly.

Exploring Regional Music
Student Activity 6

1. Answers will vary. This is entirely subjective material so allow students to express their opinions and even debate freely. They should support their opinions with logical reasoning. Explain that music is used all over the world as a tool for spiritual healing. In modern medicine, sound waves can be used to break up congestion and blockages. You may wish to explain the "placebo effect." The placebo effect is a change in a person's illness or behavior that results from a belief that the treatment will have an effect rather than from the actual treatment.

2. Music is used as a healing tool in Native American cultures from northern Canada to Tierra del Fuego; in Afro-Caribbean Santería and voodoo ceremonies; and throughout Africa, Asia, and other lands. In our own culture, certain Christian church congregations often use music, singing, or sound to enhance the effects of healing ceremonies.

Reminder: *An example of Gnawa healing music can be heard on Glencoe's "World Music: A Cultural Legacy" audio program—Disc One, Track 24 (Cassette 1, Side B).*

LESSON 7 MUSIC OF AFRICA SOUTH OF THE SAHARA

Student Worksheet

1. Possible answers: The talking drum, through its high and low pitches, communicates words and coded phrases to its listeners; oral historians called griots compose songs about historical and social events, which they then spread throughout the community; instruments such as the *mbira* (thumb piano) are used to communicate with ancestral spirits and to ask for guidance; songs are used as fables to teach social and moral lessons to children.

2. Students should describe at least two of the following African instruments:

    a. The *mbira (sanza)* is an instrument made of

metal keys suspended by a bridge over a wooden body. It is played with the thumb and forefinger of each hand.

   b. The African talking drum has a wooden body with skins on each side. The musician plays it by striking it with a curved stick while exerting pressure on the strings that connect the skins.

   c. The *balafon* is a wooden xylophone with wooden bars suspended over dried gourds

   d. The 21-string harp called the *kora* is from West Africa.

   e. The *valiha* is a tubular bamboo zither from the island of Madagascar.

   f. Trumpets and horns are made of animal horn, wood, or dried gourds.

3. Students will have created two or more rhythms played simultaneously, or a polyrhythm.

Audio Activity

TRACK 1 NIGERIA

1. The accordion was introduced to Nigerians by Europeans. It was popular in the United Kingdom, Ireland, and other European countries before it arrived in Africa.

2. Great Britain colonized Nigeria in the early 1900s.

TRACK 2 GAMBIA

1. The playing of the African harp is much more rhythmic, or percussion-like. There are no sliding notes, or "slurs." Generally, there are no chords used in West African harp music.

TRACK 3 ZIMBABWE

1. The singers are not singing the same melody. The second singer is echoing, or answering, the first singer. This is a type of "call-and-response" singing.

TRACK 4 GHANA

1. Students will hear modern Western instruments, such as the electric guitar, bass, drum set, and horns in the beginning of the song.

2. There are also African talking drums in the recording. The song is sung in the Ga language from Ghana.

TRACK 5 UGANDA

1. The male singer sings a "question" and the female singers sing their "answer." (This is called call-and-response.) The female words almost always stay the same, whereas the male verses change constantly.

TRACK 6 ETHIOPIA

1. The repeated verse that ends in "oh-oh" and the refrain "Babure-hey" are probably the parts of this piece that stand out to students.

2. The musician is strumming the strings with a wooden plectrum. If he were using his fingers, the sound of the strings would be duller.

**Exploring Regional Music
Student Activity 7**

1. Allow students to freely express their opinions, but remind them that they should support their opinions with logical arguments. There are no correct answers to these questions. Obviously, traditional storytelling and the verbal spreading of news play an important role in the lives of children or illiterate adults. News often spreads by word of mouth in local communities or within circles of friends. Modern media, on the other hand, reaches masses with great speed. You may wish to discuss the following ideas with students: Have modern people become less in touch with their neighbors and more attuned to the wider world around them? When does exposure to modern media help us perform better within our local communities, and when does it have the opposite effect?

2. Discuss with students the value of traditional customs and music. Except for Native American traditions, relatively few of which were absorbed into mainstream society, the people of the United States and Canada have no other strong indigenous traditions. The countries in this region were settled by Europeans who imposed their own values in their adopted homelands.

Reminder: *An example of* kora *music can be heard on Glencoe's "World Music: A Cultural Legacy" audio program—Disc 2, Track 2 (Cassette 2, Side A).*

LESSON 8 MUSIC OF SOUTH ASIA

Student Worksheet

1. **a.** tala
   b. raga
   c. Hindustani
   d. tamboura
2. the sitar
3. the violin
4. tabla
5. Possible answers: the interaction between raga (melody) and tala (rhythm); the use of a drone; the lack of chords; the use of improvisation in melody and rhythm; a slow introductory section called the *alap;* all instruments usually play the same melody together in unison

Audio Activity

TRACK 7   PAKISTAN

1. The chorus repeats each line sung by the lead singer. This style is called "call-and-response."
2. Answers will vary. Possible answers include rhythmic, exciting, catchy, and so on. Remind students that this is Muslim religious music. It is meant to stir the spirit to prayer and devotion to Allah. American gospel music is used in a similar fashion in the United States.

TRACK 8   INDIAN VOCAL RHYTHMS

1. Students' answers may include the following: The spoken words are very quick and smooth, unlike anything I've ever heard. It is difficult to distinguish when one person stops speaking and the other begins.
2. Possible answers: the piece and the individual parts are well rehearsed and very complicated; the musicians dart in and out of the piece in a seamless fashion; the cycles of rhythm are very complex and mathematically precise.

TRACK 9   BENGALI FOLK MUSIC

1. Answers will vary. The singer has a very flexible range. He is able to sing many notes from low to high. He has excellent breath control, allowing him to sustain notes for long periods of time. At the time of the recording, Purna Das was 55 years old.

TRACK 10   INDIAN HAMMERED DULCIMER

1. The musician raises and lowers the pitch by pushing into the drum skin. The low drum of the tabla has a slightly flexible skin. After the drummer hits the drum with his fingers, he presses the palm of his hand across the face of the skin, thereby creating a sliding sound from low to high.

TRACK 11   SOUTH INDIAN FLUTE

1. The bamboo flute and the violin are also featured in this song.
2. The flute leads each melody line, and the violin follows quickly afterward.

TRACK 12   THE SITAR

1. The *alap* helps to warm up the listener to the scale and melody.
2. The *alap* introduces the "colors" of the piece. It gets the listener in the mood for the rest of the song.
3. When the drums finally enter, they have a very dramatic presence because of their sound quality and rhythmic nature.

TRACK 13   NORTH INDIAN TABLA

1. The drums are played with the fingers and palms of each hand. Different combinations of fingers are used to play the notes so quickly.
2. There are many different drum sounds associated with the tabla. Your students may identify the three most important sounds—the dominant, ringing note played with the second finger of the right hand; the low, sliding sound of the left hand pushing into the skin; and the "swishing" sound of the fingers of the right hand as they race across the skin. Allow students to express themselves freely.

Exploring Regional Music
Student Activity 8

1. Moving the fret away from the plucked area will lower the pitch of the string. Ask your students which sound would be lower—blowing into a bottle half filled with water, or blowing into the same bottle when it is empty. Once the space inside the bottle is reduced, the pitch gets higher. The same principle applies to a string resting on a fret.

2. Since there are so many scales (based on different ragas) in Indian music, movable frets are necessary so that strings can be adjusted to match the pitches of each scale.

LESSON 9 MUSIC OF EAST ASIA

Student Worksheet

1. **a.** The 12 *lü*
   b. female = yin, male = yang
2. Possible answers: In all Western music, chords are used. In traditional Eastern music there is no concept of chords. The music is linear, and most instruments play variations of the same melody. Asian music seeks the maximum effect from the fewest sounds. There is no need to clutter a song with consistent sound or with many notes. It is felt that simplicity and skill in executing each note is most important. There may be much ornamentation such as pitch bending, sliding up and down, and quavering. The concept of rhythm is more developed in the East than it is in the West.

Audio Activity

TRACK 14 JAPANESE FLUTE

1. Possible answers: harmony, rhythm, chords

TRACK 15 JAPANESE DRUMMING

1. This piece is performed in a precise, well rehearsed manner. With so many musicians playing at the same time, the drumming rhythm is very precise. There would be no such precision if the musicians were improvising.

TRACK 16 CHINA

1. The string instruments are all playing variations of the same melody. Sometimes they may omit a note or two, but then they reenter and play slight ornamentations or variations of the main melody.
2. Two percussion instruments heard in this song are cymbals and wood clapper (wood block).

TRACK 17 KOREA

1. Silk strings produce a denser, duller sound than steel strings. The sound delay of silk is much shorter than with metal. Metal strings sound brighter and lighter.

TRACK 18 TIBET

1. This is Tibetan overtone singing. All the monks are singing only one, low note. The monks, though, use subtle movements and changes in their throat cavities to produce several other notes. Also, there is an "air" sound that seems to expand and contract in swirls.

Exploring Regional Music
Student Activity 9

1. *Taiko* drumming has been associated with mystical powers. It has been used to facilitate communication with the gods. *Shakuhachi* music was developed as a way to practice meditation and concentration. This type of flute music brings the player and listener to a state of peace and stillness.
2. There is a strong, steady beat in *taiko* music, but a general lack of rhythm in *shakuhachi* music. *Taiko* drumming is very loud and intense, whereas *shakuhachi* music is soft and gentle. *Taiko* is performed in ensembles; *shakuhachi* is often performed solo.

Reminder: *An example of* taiko *drumming can be heard on Glencoe's "World Music: A Cultural Legacy" audio program–Disc 2, Track 15 (Cassette 2, Side A). An example of the solo* shakuhachi *flute can be heard on Glencoe's "World Music: A Cultural Legacy" audio program–Disc 2, Track 14 (Cassette 2, Side A).*

LESSON 10 MUSIC OF SOUTHEAST ASIA

Student Worksheet

1. The Philippines is a Christian (Catholic) nation. The island of Bali is Hindu.
2. This is done with movable bridges, which change the tension points in the suspended string and thus alter the pitch. Similar effects are achieved through the use of movable frets

in North Africa, the Middle East, India, and throughout South Asia and other areas.

3. northern Vietnam (*chau van* possession ceremonies); Sumatra (spirit songs to communicate through mediums)

4. Trance is an important element of religion throughout Africa, Asia, Latin America (through African traditions), Australia (Aborigines), the islands of Oceania, and even among some American religious groups. Allow your students to speculate freely and direct them to the premise that where tribal and ancestral religions were supplanted and dominated by Christianity, Islam, and other organized religions, instances of spirit worship and trance are greatly diminished.

Audio Activity

TRACK 19   THE *KHENE* FROM LAOS

1. Possible answers: accordion, harmonica
2. Yes, there is a constant note (drone) being played throughout the song; this is characteristic of the *khene*.

TRACK 20   VIETNAMESE FOLK MUSIC

1. Possible answers include: serious, inquisitive, insightful, thoughtful, and so on. It seems neither happy nor sad, yet there is a seriousness about it.

TRACK 21   JAVANESE GAMELAN

1. The piece slows down in rhythm dramatically and incrementally as it approaches the ending.
2. The final low note on the largest gong seems to provide closure to the piece.

TRACK 22   DRUMMING FROM VIETNAM

1. The rhythm is not a steady, fixed beat. It alternates in patterns.
2. Occasionally the musician hits the sticks against each other and against the rims of the drums.

TRACK 23   CAMBODIA

1. wooden xylophone, drum, flute, bowed fiddle

TRACK 24   LAOTIAN FOLK MUSIC

1. Students may correctly guess that the dance movements associated with this style of music incorporate swaying from side to side, moving the hips, alternating movement of the feet from one beat to the next, waving the hands, twisting the arms, and clapping hands.

Exploring Regional Music
Student Activity 10

1. There is no conductor in a gamelan orchestra. All the musicians sit facing the same direction. The gamelan performers take their cues from the lead drummer.

2. These instruments are extremely cumbersome and require setup and preparation. Gamelan are also heavy and would be difficult to transport. The irregular shapes of the instruments would require individual custom-made cases to protect them from damage during transport. The weight of the instruments would increase the costs of shipping and handling.

Reminder: *An example of gamelan music can be heard on Glencoe's "World Music: A Cultural Legacy" audio program–Disc 2, Track 21 (Cassette 2, Side B).*

LESSON 11   MUSIC OF AUSTRALIA AND OCEANIA

Student Worksheet

1. The most direct correlation is the Native American powwow, at which Native American groups from different regions gather to compete in song and dance. Your students might also be reminded of local talent contests, music festivals, and other music-based social events.

2. Music in Aboriginal Australia relates journeys and actions of ancestor beings who are believed to have created all things on the earth. In this way, it plays an active role in the regeneration and continuance of life on earth. Westerners use music mostly for recreation and relaxation, and sometimes expression.

3. Answers will vary. Group singing in the West occurs at religious ceremonies of worship, at home with family members to celebrate holidays or special events (Christmas, birthdays, anniversaries, and so on), and to some degree at organized public events such as protests, demonstrations, and concerts.

4. In societies where the family unit is more integrated and people spend more time in the presence of one another, music tends to be a group function rather than performance-based. Encourage your students to speculate further about this issue.

Audio Activity

TRACK 25   AUSTRALIAN FUSION

1. The song opens with solo drums. The rhythm is slow and steady. The didgeridoo has a fierce, barking sound. The synthesizer is emitting a sound similar to human voices.

TRACK 26   SAMOA

1. The women call and the men respond. This is a "call-and-response" style of singing, common in Africa and other parts of the world.

TRACK 27   FOLK MUSIC FROM VANUATU

1. Answers will vary. Images may include people in tropical costumes wearing flowers in their hair and grass skirts. Their mood would be happy, with lots of smiling faces and children nearby. They might be on a beach, under palm trees, and so on.

2. Students may realize that they have seen images of these islands in the media—on television, in travel brochures, and in magazines. Have students debate the following question: Does modern media affect our ability to experience other cultures without prejudging and categorizing them?

TRACK 28   THE DIDGERIDOO

1. The didgeridoo has an otherworldly type of sound. Because the musician opens and closes his mouth and throat cavities while playing, the sound can be compressed (thin) or open (thick). The air swirls around in the tube relative to the mouth movements of the musician. The "barking" sounds are sharp puffs of air accompanied by singing into the tube.

2. Because the instrument is an extension of the human body and breath, students may think it is a good tool for communicating with ancestor spirits.

TRACK 29   AUSTRALIAN FOLK MUSIC

1. Possible answers: The musicians would be dressed informally, perhaps as cowboys. The fiddle, guitar, and bouncy rhythm evoke images of a tavern or barn dance.

2. This music sounds similar to North American folk, hoedown, and country music. All these types of music evolved from the same British and Celtic folk source.

**Exploring Regional Music
Student Activity 11**

1. A never-ending supply of breath and the human life force no doubt carry special significance. Nose breath is considered sacred among many traditional societies, and air used to play the didgeridoo is inhaled only through the nose. It is not clear how this style of breathing developed among the Aborigines, and whether it was created for only practical and/or spiritual purposes. Allow students to speculate.

2. Drones are used for concentration, meditation, and prayer in most traditional societies. They are essential in devotional music from India, other parts of Asia, and even in the West, where they appeared in ancient liturgical music.

Reminder: *An example of didgeridoo music can be heard on Glencoe's "World Music: A Cultural Legacy" audio program—Disc 2, Track 28 (Cassette 2, Side B).*

Teacher Notes

World Music: A Cultural Legacy

Teacher Notes

Teacher Notes

Teacher Notes

Teacher Notes

Teacher Notes